Mastering Basic Math Skills

Games for Kindergarten Through Second Grade

Bonnie Adama Britt

NATIONAL COUNCIL OF
TEACHERS OF MATHEMATICS

www.nctm.org/more4u
Access code: MBM14307

Copyright © 2014 by
The National Council of Teachers of Mathematics, Inc.
1906 Association Drive, Reston, VA 20191-1502
(703) 620-9840; (800) 235-7566; www.nctm.org
All rights reserved
First printing 2014

Library of Congress Cataloging-in-Publication Data

Britt, Bonnie Adama, author.
  Mastering basic math skills. Games for kindergarten through second grade / by Bonnie Adama
Britt.
    pages cm
  ISBN 978-0-87353-757-5
  1. Games in mathematics education. 2. Mathematics--Study and teaching (Early childhood)--Activity programs. 3. Early childhood education--Activity programs. I. Title. II. Title: Games for kindergarten through second grade.
  QA20.G35B75 2014
  372.7'049--dc23
                        2013033812

The National Council of Teachers of Mathematics is the public voice of mathematics education, supporting teachers to ensure equitable mathematics learning of the highest quality for all students through vision, leadership, professional development, and research.

Printed in the United States of America

Table of Contents

Preface v

Acknowledgments vii

About Math Games

Why Use Math Games? 1

Parents Using Math Games 3

Teachers Using Math Games 7

Using the Games 15

The Games

Number Recognition and Counting 19

Comparing Numbers to 10 33

Addition 49

Place Value 103

Multidigit Addition 119

Subtraction 137

Multiple Operations in One Game 159

Multiplication 179

Money 191

Fractions 213

References 220

I tried to teach my child with books.
He only gave me puzzled looks.
I tried to teach my child with words.
They passed him by, unheard.
In despair I turned aside.
"How will I teach my child?" I cried.
Into my hand he put the key . . .
"Come" he said, "and play with me."

—Unknown

Preface

I have a confession to make. I was one of those kids who never considered using the words *math* and *fun* in the same sentence! I struggled to understand math; I certainly didn't consider myself to be successful at it; I can't remember ever enjoying a single moment of it (probably a mild understatement!), and I avoided it like the plague in college!

Then, suddenly, I was an elementary school teacher, and I had to teach math! Well, how hard could it be? I only had to teach up to third grade math. I had managed to memorize the multiplication facts. What about fractions? The thought of multiplying fractions terrified me. No, you don't have to multiply fractions in the third grade. Whew! I was pretty sure I could do this!

I quickly realized that I was teaching math the way it had been taught to me in elementary school. Even though I had been an elementary education major in college, there had been no classes on how children learn math and how it should be taught. (Unfortunately, I think the situation is only a little better today.)

Needless to say, I was uninspired and uninspiring. I wasn't an effective math teacher, and neither my students nor I were in any way captivated by, or fascinated with, math. I decided that this status quo was not acceptable. I didn't want to repeat the past. I wanted to be a good teacher and I wanted my students to love math! I had heard that was possible, although you certainly couldn't prove it by me! I had a lot of math to learn and a long way to go before I could teach it well.

I began by spending an entire summer at a math institute for elementary school teachers at the University of California at Riverside. Math started to become understandable. It was definitely challenging, exciting, and, yes (gasp!), fun! Who knew? All right, that was all well and good, but I realized that the journey had only just begun. I began work on a Master of Arts in Elementary Education at California State University at San Bernardino. My particular emphasis was on brain-based learning—how children learn and what that means regarding how they should be taught. I packed two years of course work into just five years! That's what happens when you are teaching full-time and working on a master's degree.

I read everything I could get my hands on about how children learn math and how to teach math in engaging and effective ways. As I learned, I began to change the way I taught. One of the things I realized was how very important it is to listen to and learn from the children—they are great teachers!

Much changed in my math classroom. One of the learning tools I began to experiment with was math games. As I watched the students play, I quickly realized that games were a wonderful, useful teaching tool.

In the years since I retired, I have worked in elementary schools all over southern California helping teachers, parents, students, administrators, and after-school child-care workers use math games to support their children in learning and practicing math concepts and skills. Their enthusiasm for these games as a teaching tool encouraged me to compile them, including their education rationales and some pointers I have picked up from playing the games with children.

The games in this book will provide children with—

- engaging opportunities to discover math concepts;
- stimulating math reinforcement; and
- the chance to discover that math can be fun and not threatening or frustrating.

For parents and teachers, the games offer another effective and engaging way to help their children.

The best part is that parents, teachers, and children will enjoy playing the games in this book. So, get everyone together and start playing! Have fun!

More4U

Many of the games in this book use materials such as cards, number lines, recording sheets, and game boards. These can all be found for downloading and printing on NCTM's More4U online resource. Simply go to www.nctm.org/more4U and enter the access code that is on the title page of this book.

Acknowledgments

After many years in the elementary classroom, I can say without any doubt that my students taught me more about how to teach than anyone else. I had no idea that was going to happen when I stepped into the classroom on the first morning of my teaching career. After all, I was the teacher and they were the learners. As it turned out, we were all learners.

So, thank you to Marcie (a second grader) who taught me that she was just as capable of answering a question as I was. Thank you to Brandon (a first grader) who pointed out five different and perfectly legitimate ways to solve an addition challenge. Thanks to the entire third grade who became so excited about solving a multiplication challenge that I couldn't get a word in edgewise. And that was as it should have been!

Thanks to Betty and John Clemens, my mathematics and writing mentors, who took a great deal of their precious time to question me, listen to me, read what I wrote, and nudge me in the right direction.

I will forever be grateful for my good friend, teaching partner, and fellow learner Carolyn Oleson.

Nelson Togerson was the very best principal a teacher could have. He knew how children learned and understood how they should be taught. Thanks, Nelson, for all you did to help me become a better teacher.

Thanks to my excellent editor, Maryanne Bannon, for her expertise and patience.

I will be forever grateful to Myrna Jacobs, the publications manager at NCTM. She knows that using games is an effective way to engage children in mathematics. Thank you, Myrna, for finding me and giving me this exciting challenge and opportunity.

And last, but definitely not least, thanks to my husband, Rex, for new beginnings, wonderful surprises, warm love, a constructive critical eye, insightful questions, and ongoing support and encouragement. He's a good cook, too!

About Math Games

Why Use Math Games?

There are some who think (wrongly) that teaching math games to children is a waste of valuable educational time. After years of teaching math to children and using games, I am convinced that math games are an immensely helpful resource for parents and teachers who want to make sure that their children develop and practice some of the skills they will need to become proficient with math in school and in life.

The benefits of using math games with children are many:

1. Games create a context for developing and supporting children's mathematical understanding and reasoning. They—

   * help children learn important mathematical skills and processes with understanding. That is, children do not just memorize rules but gain true knowledge of the concepts and processes. Understanding develops through interaction with materials, peers, parents, and teachers in settings where children have opportunities to discover and use number relationships.
   * require a variety of problem-solving skills. They help students develop the ability to think critically and solve problems. While playing a game, children eagerly make and test hypotheses, create strategies, think and plan ahead, and organize information.
   * are particularly effective in helping children make sense of how numbers work.
   * encourage strategic thinking. As children play math games, they develop mental strategies to compete successfully, understand the objectives, evaluate their own (and their opponents') strengths and weaknesses, learn routine procedures and probabilities, keep track of what is going on, and make short- and long-range plans.
   * provoke children into debating, explaining, and thinking. Children learn from discussing, sharing, and reflecting throughout game sessions. The interaction required by games improves their ability to communicate and use mathematical language.

2. Through playing and analyzing games, children gain computational fluency.

   Math is like a ladder. If you miss a step, sometimes you can't go on. Elementary school provides a crucial window of opportunity for students to master certain skills in math. Students who haven't grasped certain mathematical concepts and skills by the end of elementary school are more likely to have problems in middle school, high school, and beyond.

   Games are an effective and engaging way to help children in kindergarten through second grade achieve mastery of basic facts. This means that children are able to give a quick response (in three seconds or less) without resorting to an inefficient computational strategy such as counting. Computational fluency plays a key role in helping children successfully work with higher-level math problems.

3. Games motivate children.

   Math games are inherently interesting, and because they are stimulating, intriguing, challenging, and fun, games motivate children to work at a task over and over again.

   Peggy Kaye (1987, p. 236), in her book *Games for Math*, put it perfectly when she said, "Games put children in exactly the right frame of mind for learning difficult things. Children relax when they play—and they concentrate. They don't mind repeating certain facts or procedures over and over, if repetition is part of the game. Children throw themselves into playing games the way they never throw themselves into filling out workbook pages. And games can, if you select the right ones, help children learn almost everything they need to master in elementary math."

4. Math games encourage parent involvement.

Games offer an effective and pleasant way for parents to help their children learn math by doing one of the things kids love—playing games. Parents appreciate the fact that there's no nagging or pressuring when a math game is proposed.

5. Games offer many opportunities for parents and teachers to discover their children's strengths and weaknesses.

Parents and teachers who observe and interact with their children while playing math games can discover a great deal about what they know and can do in math. Games provide feedback so that parents, teachers, and the children know what they have done well and what they need to practice.

6. Math games promote confidence and positive attitudes toward math.

They help children master not only mathematical skills, principles, and concepts but also to appreciate and enjoy math. Math games almost always motivate, excite, and challenge children.

7. Games meet the needs of diverse learners.

Because math games require active involvement, use concrete objects (sometimes called manipulatives by elementary teachers), and are hands-on, they offer multisensory support and are ideal for all learners. Games reinforce and sharpen the math skills and concepts of children who are already good at math, and they stimulate, strengthen, and empower children who need extra help. Games cut across ages and genders. Players of widely varying abilities can have fun playing and learning together.

8. Math games teach life skills.

On the social level, game playing can help children learn to work cooperatively, give and take praise and criticism, instruct others, and accept success and failure in the presence of peers. In the process of playing a game, children may develop initiative, interest, curiosity, resourcefulness, independence, and responsibility. Plus, as children play, they further their development of hand-eye coordination, concentration levels, visual discrimination, and memory.

To sum up, math games—

- make children more open to learning;
- motivate them to keep practicing new skills;
- help children remember what they learn; and
- teach or reinforce many of the skills that a formal curriculum teaches, plus a skill that math lessons sometimes unwisely leave out—the skill of having fun with math, of thinking hard and enjoying it.

Parents Using Math Games

It's common knowledge that young children whose parents read to them have a tremendous advantage in school. But did you know that you might also help your child learn mathematics at home? Research by Greg J. Duncan and Amy Claessens (2007, pp. 1428–46) shows that early math skills may very well be a better predictor of academic success than reading ability.

As my teaching career progressed, I frequently saw that children no longer memorized their addition facts or multiplication tables. With the math curriculum as extensive as it is, teachers cannot afford to take the time to ensure that students learn the basic facts (sad, but true). Parents are partners in the process, and you can assure your children greater opportunities to succeed in math if you support their learning the basics at home. Games fit the bill wonderfully!

Math games for children and families are the perfect way to reinforce and extend the skills children learn at school. They are one of the most effective ways that parents can develop their child's math skills without lecturing or applying pressure. When studying math, there's an element of repetition that's an important part of learning new concepts and developing automatic recall of math facts. Number facts (remember those times tables?) can be boring and tedious to learn and practice. A game can generate an enormous amount of practice—practice that does not have kids complaining about how much work they have to do. What better way to master number facts than by playing an interesting game?

Helping your child get better at math doesn't have to be difficult, painful, or scary. Don't be fooled—just because games are fun doesn't mean they are frivolous. We tend to think that when children are playing, they aren't learning and vice versa. But children do learn through play, and having fun can even help them learn more effectively.

In the process of playing a game, your child may develop initiative, interest, curiosity, resourcefulness, independence, and responsibility. Would that happen with a problem-packed worksheet, workbook page, or flashcards?

As you join your child in these games, you will begin to perceive your child's strengths and weaknesses in math and know what he or she will need to practice. Any game can be changed to meet the needs of your child. Don't hesitate to go back to a game if you know your child needs to practice a particular skill.

Resources for Parents

The National PTA (http://www.pta.org) has provided *Parents' Guides for Student Success* at every grade level. These guides are based on the new Common Core State Standards, and provide an overview of the key skills your child should learn by the end of their present grade in language arts and mathematics. The Internet links to specific grade level content are provided in the Reference section on page 220.

Many of the games use special materials such as cards, game boards, and recording sheets. You can download them for printing by visiting NCTM's online resource at www.nctm.org/more4u. The access code can be found on the title page of this book.

Everyone can have fun

Your family will have fun together, too. Not so long ago, I had a mother tell me that her entire family (two parents and three children) had a enjoyable evening playing a particular math game. After the children went to bed, the parents continued to play!

Remember that card games are *games* (that is, they should be fun!). If pleasure is not connected to the game, children will be unwilling to play, and little learning will take place. Games are effective as teaching aids only as long as they are entertaining and parents and children enjoy playing them together. You are investing time in something that can bring hours of pleasurable interaction—and learning math is an immense fringe benefit!

As the Internet continues to play a larger role in education, a growing number of online sites host free math games, most of which are challenging, exciting, fun, and age appropriate. That's all well and good, but above all else, children crave time with their parents. Because learning is a social process, children learn best through enjoyable games and activities that involve interaction with other people.

Indulge your children with your undivided attention, and play a math game. A price cannot be put on the quality of the time you will have spent with them. They will have fun learning, and they will remember those times with greater fondness than the hours they spent playing educational computer games.

When playing math games with your children your primary responsibility is to be enthusiastic and eager to play. Your second responsibility is to ask your children questions—questions that will encourage them to think and to verbalize what they are doing and why.

Asking questions

While playing a game, children don't always know what to do next. Here are a few good questions to help them begin to help themselves and not to rely on you, the parent, to give them the answer. As parents, we need to ask our children good questions to promote the kind of thinking they require to give good answers. Questions encourage reflection and help children make mathematical connections. Ask your children, "What can you do to help yourself?"

- Use your fingers to count?
- Count the dots on the dice or cards?
- Use counters (beans, paper clips, pennies, and such) to figure it out?
- Draw a picture or diagram?
- Start with something you already know?

Example
"If you know that five plus five equals ten, how can that help you know what five plus six equals?"

Be curious about how your child solves problems. Ask questions to understand their thinking. Here are a few more great questions to ask when playing a game:

- What card do you need?
- Which cards would not be helpful?
- Can you prove to me that a _____ is what you need?
- Why do you think that?
- How did you know to try that strategy?
- How do you know you have the right answer?
- Will this work with every number? Every similar situation?
- When will this strategy not work? Can you give me an example?
- What did you notice while playing the game?

> "Convince me that you are right" or "prove it" are not challenges, but are requests that can be used with children to encourage them to think more deeply and articulate the concepts they are using. At first, children find it difficult to respond, but the more often they explain what they are thinking, the more competent they become.

When I demonstrate how to play a game or I play a game with a child, I often think out loud: "Hmm, if I use a five, that will get me closer to ten than if I used a four." Children then "hear" what I am thinking, which helps them understand why I decided to play as I did. Perhaps it was a strategy that had not occurred to them.

I know it is very challenging for parents (or any adult) not to give a child an answer. However, when you give a child the answer, who is solving the problem? Ask questions that will prompt them to do the thinking.

Recording sheets

Many of the games include recording sheets. Writing down the problems solved while playing a math game can be helpful to you and your child. You will be able to note any strengths or weaknesses over a period of time and to see the growth and development of your child's math abilities, and your child can feel a sense of accomplishment when looking at all the completed math work. When you begin a game with a recording sheet, have your child put the date at the top for easier comparisons later on.

Calculators

The calculator can be a valuable tool if a child understands the basic mathematical ideas, concepts, and meanings. Each child should learn to solve problems by using mental and written calculations as well as a calculator. Even young children can use calculators to focus on the mathematical ideas behind computation rather than just on the act of calculating.

Use your judgment as to whether calculators will speed up or defeat the purpose of the game. If a calculator eliminates the thought process, it's not appropriate for that situation.

You can play math games anytime, anywhere

Wherever you go, you can carry a small zip-tight plastic bag containing a deck of cards, two dice, a small notebook (for keeping scores), and a pencil. Games can be played while traveling in the car or on an airplane, or waiting for—

- the car to be serviced;
- your order to arrive in a restaurant;
- the movie to start; and
- appointments at the doctor's or dentist's office.

Be assured that what you do to encourage your child's success in mathematics matters. Nothing affects the academic outcome for a child as much as the involvement of a parent.

Math games aren't just prescriptions for children struggling with math or needing a little more practice or looking for something to do. Pick a math game that sounds like fun. Grab a deck of cards or some dice, and invite your child to play for fifteen minutes. That's it! It's a quick and easy way to make a huge difference in your child's math abilities. Your child will get better at math, become more confident, and want to learn—and play—even more.

Teachers Using Math Games

Game playing hasn't been a traditional part of the math classroom. If a teacher did use a game, it was played in the last ten minutes on Friday or as a rainy-day recess activity. Occasionally, a teacher might use a math game in a small-group learning center or as a reward for finishing work. Games were considered to be frivolous and a waste of valuable time. This idea is quickly changing.

Teachers and administrators are beginning to realize that using games as part of math instruction provides many benefits. Math games—

- reinforce mathematical objectives and meet many of the kindergarten through second grade Common Core State Standards for Mathematics;
- are easily linked to and can supplement any mathematics textbook;
- are repeatable (reuse often and sustain interest and engagement);
- can be open-ended, allowing for multiple approaches;
- are easy to prepare;
- increase curiosity and motivation;
- establish a sense of community among the students;
- create a student-centered learning environment;
- reduce anxiety in the mathematics classroom;
- allow for cooperative learning opportunities;
- inherently differentiate learning;
- build strategy and reasoning skills;
- engage individual learners simultaneously;
- lead students to talk about mathematics; and
- compel players to work mentally.

Planning games for the classroom

Once students have been introduced to a new math concept and they have begun to understand it, they need to practice it. That's when games become appropriate and can enhance the learning experience.

When planning a game for the classroom, there are four simple steps to follow:

1. Make sure that you play the game with someone (spouse, your own kids, in grade-level teams) to gain familiarity with its rules and subtleties. Determine whether the rules need to be modified to meet the needs of your students.

2. Consider how you will teach the game to your class:
   - You can play the game against the whole class.
   - Two students could demonstrate while you explain.
   - One student can play the game with you.

3. As you demonstrate how a game is played, think out loud so the children understand the strategy you might be using; for example, "I need to get as close to twenty as I can. If I use my five, I'll be closer to twenty than if I use my four."

4. Allow enough time to demonstrate the game or to remind the students how it is played and to let them settle in and play the game. (Fifteen minutes probably won't be adequate.) Remember that playing a game for the first time requires a period of learning and clarification. As students become more familiar with the game, they will spend less time checking the rules and more time exploring mathematical ideas and developing strategies.

Helpful tips when using math games

- Be very deliberate about pairing students or forming small groups who will be playing the game on their own. To learn a game, pair students who are similar but not quite equal in their math understandings. Once children know a game, partner children at equal skill levels. Partnering students of dissimilar skill levels may sound like a good idea, but one of them is often very quickly bored, and the other may just give up. In addition, some students often think intuitively and cannot always explain the why or how of what they did. If a pair of children cannot explain their thinking to each other, then they cannot learn from each other.

- Use games for specific purposes, not as time fillers. Know what mathematical objective and Common Core standard will be met by playing the game.

- Play the games repeatedly. The only exception to this rule is a game that is too easy for everyone. However, over the years, I have discovered that games I thought might be too easy were often a challenge. Children do not begin to build strategies, plan ahead, or problem solve unless they have played a game several times.

- Don't hesitate to go back to a skill and play a game if you know the students need to practice it, even if the text has taken you on to something else.

- To keep all players engaged, make sure they are taking turns, paying attention to the game, and checking their partner's work. Because you cannot be everywhere at once, players need to keep each other accountable. I have students initial the other player's work if it is correct before they can take their turn. If it is not correct, players return the recording sheets to their partners and kindly suggest that they recalculate.

- Calculators can be quite helpful for settling questions about answers, executing complex calculations, or keeping track of players' cumulative scores. Use your judgment as to whether calculators will speed up or defeat the purpose of the game. If a calculator eliminates the thought process, it's not appropriate for that situation.

- Many of the games include recording sheets. Recording the problems solved while playing a math game can leave a mathematical trail that is of great value to children, teachers, and parents. Children can feel a sense of accomplishment as they look back at all the math work they have done; teachers can use the records for assessment; and parents will appreciate this "evidence" that their children are actually doing mathematics and not just "playing games."

- Make sure all students are doing their own calculating or keeping their own scores. Every once in a while I have discovered that one person on the team is keeping all the scores. In that case, only that student is thinking and doing the math.

- Most of the games in this book have been designed as competitive matches where the high scorer wins. They can all be transformed into games where the high scorer is not the winner or into noncompetitive activities. One of the ways this can be done is to have one of the players roll a die. If the number rolled is an even number, the player with the greatest answer or score is the winner. If the number rolled is an odd number, the player with the least answer or score is the winner. Many of the games can be played in such a way that players keep track of and try to improve their scores over a period of days. Children can enjoy keeping graphs of this information themselves.

- Have fun together. If pleasure is not connected to the game, children will be unwilling to play and little learning will take place.

- Sending a letter to parents that tells them how and why math games will be used in your classroom is a good idea. It can allay any doubts that may arise when their children come home describing how they "played games during math today!"

Math games and teacher responsibilities

Assessment

Good games evaluate children's progress. Children's thinking often becomes apparent through the actions and decisions they make during a game. Assessment is the process of drawing reasonable inferences about what a student knows by evaluating what they say and do while playing the game. Games provide feedback so that both teachers and the children know what they have done well and what they need to practice.

Once a game is fairly familiar to children, move from group to group, listening and questioning. Make dated anecdotal records on which game is being played, what skill or concept is being practiced, and how each child is progressing. Not only does this help in assessing the children's strengths and weaknesses but it also allows you to differentiate instruction.

The recording sheets that children produce while playing games can be placed in assessment portfolios, creating a paper trail as evidence of mathematical development that can be of great value to children, teachers, and parents. When beginning a game with a recording sheet, children should put their names and the date at the top of the paper.

Finally, games provide children with a powerful way of assessing their own mathematical abilities. The immediate feedback children receive from their peers while playing games can help them evaluate their mathematical concepts and revise inefficient, inadequate, or erroneous ones.

Communication

While the students are playing the game, you should be moving from group to group listening to their conversations, asking them questions, and insisting on high quality communications among students. You should be modeling to the students the kind of questions you expect them to ask each other by your own probing questions:

- What card do you need?
- Which cards would not be helpful?
- Can you prove to me that a ___ is what you need?
- Why do you think that?
- How did you know to try that strategy?
- Will this work with every number? Every similar situation?
- When will this strategy not work? Can you give an example?
- Who has a different strategy?
- How is your answer the same as or different from (another student's)?
- Can you repeat your classmate's ideas in your own words?
- Do you agree or disagree with your classmate's idea? Why?

"Convince me that you are right" or "prove it" are not challenges but requests that can be used with children at any time. At first, children find it difficult to respond, but the more they explain what they are thinking, the more competent they become.

Too often players are willing to give their partners the answer, unwittingly sabotaging them and making it possible for some players to do no thinking whatsoever. Not good! Children need to be encouraged to help each other by asking questions. Every time you ask a question, you are modeling the kind of questions they should be asking each other:

- What can you do to help yourself?
- Could you use your fingers to count?
- Could you count the dots on the dice or cards?
- Would counters (buttons, paper clips, and so on) help you to figure it out?
- Could you draw a picture?
- Can you start with something you already know?

Example
"If you know that five times six equals thirty, how can that help you know what six times six equals?"

I know that it is very challenging for teachers not to give a child an answer. However, when you give a child the answer, who is solving the problem? Ask questions that will prompt them to think. Good questions promote reflection and help children make mathematical connections.

Differentiating instruction

It doesn't take long for most teachers to discover that their classrooms are filled with a diversity of students with varying abilities, learning styles, learning disabilities, and facilities with the English language.

Consider the complexity of games and the thinking skills involved, and adjust the games to encourage thought at various levels if necessary. After you have done some initial assessment, you may find that some students need to keep playing the game at its simplest level, while others need to move on to the variation, which is usually a more complex version of the game, or on to another game. Games in this book are arranged from the simplest to the more complex.

Classroom management

After years of playing math games with children from kindergarten to sixth grade, I have discovered that a tough love policy (that is, no second chances) works best. I explain the game and the rules (for example, no throwing of materials, no arguing, and so forth). If a student breaks a rule, that student is immediately out of the game and must complete a worksheet or workbook page. Because that is not nearly as much fun as playing a game, discipline is immediately under control because most children will behave appropriately so they can play the game.

Here are a few suggestions I have found to work well:

- Many people think that a quiet room is one in which learning is taking place. I definitely disagree with that theory! Learning and understanding mathematics depends on communication (listening *and* talking). When children are playing games in cooperative groups, they need to be able to talk with each other. These conversations can be very constructive if children take responsibility to make sure that all players in a game understand the operations, concepts, and facts being used within the game. Sharing a variety of strategies with each other leads to fluency with numbers and helps everyone see different ways to play. The bottom line: Teach each other and learn from each other.

- You have nineteen students on a day when you want to play a math game. *Never sit down to play a game with the unpaired student.* If you do so, you have immediately lost control of what is going on while the children are playing, and you have no opportunity to listen, ask questions, or do assessments. Instead, make a group of three to play the game.

- Play on the floor—spread out so each team has its own space. (If playing on the floor is simply not an option, be sure to separate the groups as best as you can.) This will help with discipline and noise level, and materials will not get mixed up. Partners need to interact with each other, but do not need to talk to others around them, which is what happens when they play at their desks. I've found that once children of any age know this rule, they do not complain. They want to play.

- Because they are playing on the floor, it helps if each student has a clipboard for recording sheets, keeping their own scores, or drawing a picture or diagram.

- One task I model for every single game is how to decide who goes first (paper-rock-scissors, highest or lowest number on the die , birth date, and so forth). If play order is not absolutely clear, some children will spend the entire game time arguing about who goes first.

- Keep the number of players between two and four, so that turns come around quickly. It is very helpful to pair two children against two children. That way they can discuss possible strategies with each other. Two brains are almost always better than one!

- The first time your students play a math game, I guarantee you will wonder why you ever thought this would be a good idea! Some level of chaos will reign. Don't worry; move from group to group quickly, putting out the fires. Don't forget the tough love. The second time they play the game, it will be much better, and the third time it will be great!

- Never allow children to insult another player. They may disagree with answers and ideas, but not people.

- When using dice, give each team a large, heavy-duty paper plate on which to roll the dice. Not only does this muffle the sound but it effectively acts as a boundary for the dice. If the dice do not stay in the paper plate, that player loses a turn (another example of tough love). Every classroom has one or more of the how-far-I-can-throw-these-dice experimenters!

After the game

In order for students to learn from games, there are several tasks the teacher should keep in mind: Help the children focus on specific number concepts; ask them what strategies they are using; and encourage them to talk about their discoveries. Talking about the mathematics they are doing gives students the chance to clarify their thinking.

Always bring the children together to discuss what happened when they played the game. Interaction with each other helps children verbalize their thoughts, get feedback for their thinking, and hear other points of view. While you were watching them play the game, you may have noticed that some of them were using strategies that are worth sharing with the entire class. Realizing that there are different ways to approach a problem or to strategize about a process broadens learning opportunities. Students learn from one another as well as from their teachers.

Make notes on a clean copy of the game—what went well, what needed to be changed, and so forth. Put it with the math unit you are presenting; then next year, when you're ready to play, you won't have to reinvent that wheel.

Math games as homework

Math games for homework are not only the perfect way to reinforce and extend the skills children learn at school but they also encourage parents' involvement in their child's development. I have found that sending home a game already learned in class as homework for children to play with their parents is useful and welcomed by most parents. It helps give parents a sense of what can be learned from math games that are not based on workbooks or worksheets.

Every Friday I sent home a game with the students. (Each year, with the first game, I also sent a deck of ten-frame cards and two dice that were to be kept in a safe place because they would be needed throughout the school year.) My initial letter to parents included these points:

- Talk to each other while playing the games. Ask your child questions such as: "How can you figure out the answer?" "What card do you need?" "Which cards would not be helpful?" "Prove to me that a ___ is what you need" or "convince me that ___ is the right answer." Children learn from talking, sharing, and reflecting throughout game times.
- Give your child opportunities to change the games. The rules and instructions for the games are meant to be flexible. Allow your child to think of ways to change the equipment or rules. Encourage him or her to make a game easier or harder or to invent new games.
- Play the games many times over the next week. Children begin to build and practice strategies (for example, planning their moves in advance) only when the game is repeated often.
- Playing it just once or twice is not very helpful, unless the game is too easy for your child. If it's too easy or too hard, change it.
- Have fun together. If pleasure is not connected to the game, children will be unwilling to play, and little learning will take place.

A response form was included with every game, and it was the only thing due back the following Friday.

Parent Response to the Game

- What did you think of this game? Did you like it? Why or why not?

- Was this game too easy, too hard, or just right? How did you change it to meet the needs of your child?

- What do you think your child learned from playing this game?

- What did you learn about your child while playing this game? What are your child's strengths? What does he or she need to practice?

Many parents took the form very seriously, and I learned a great deal about the children's interests, strong points, and weaknesses.

I quickly discovered that if I did not respond to the completed parent form, the parents stopped returning them. They (mistakenly) assumed that I did not care. So, I began writing brief notes on the completed forms asking questions or making statements. Often it was just a "Thank you" or "This was helpful to me!" returned to the parents on the following Monday.

Evaluating math games

The National Council of Teachers of Mathematics (NCTM) believes that games can be effective tools for helping children understand math concepts and for practicing needed math skills. In terms of evaluating games for use with children, it states on its website (www.nctm.org):

> While we may jump at the opportunity to use math games as a way to engage today's learners, we must still be careful in evaluating them as effective means for teaching and learning. Some questions that might help you determine the value of a math game follow:
>
> - Is there variety in the mathematical tasks? If you play the same game over, will you be asked different questions? Are there different pathways to the end?
>
> - Are there opportunities to develop strategy while engaging in NCTM's Process Standards—problem solving, reasoning and proof, communication, connections, and representation?
>
> - Is there a combination of chance and choice in the game? That is, are there both a random component (rolling a dice, drawing a card) and an opportunity to make a decision?
>
> - Is the competition positive and nonthreatening?
>
> - Is there embedded scaffolding? If a player gets stuck, are there hints?
>
> - Are there suggestions to integrate the game into the classroom? Are there follow-up questions for teachers? Is there a way for teachers to track student progress?
>
> - Is the length of play appropriate for classroom use?
>
> - Was the math situated in a meaningful context? Does the game promote deeper understanding of mathematical concepts that is meaningful to the student?
>
> - Do the students feel empowered and in control? In other words, do decisions have clear outcomes?
>
> - Was clear feedback provided during each turn? Was the computation of scoring clear?
>
> - Does the game encourage social play? The three Cs of game playing are: competition, collaboration, and communication. Even one-player games can spark rich discussion of strategy.

A few final words

Almost every elementary school teacher struggles to find productive ways to encourage students to understand and master basic math concepts and facts. Math games meet the varied needs of learners, offer opportunities to differentiate instruction, and are effective, motivational, and engaging.

Whether you are a new teacher, a teacher new to teaching math at a different grade level, or a veteran teacher looking for a fresh perspective, I would encourage you to give math games a try. Games engage children and enhance their math learning.

Using the Games

Each game gives children practice with a particular math concept or skill, or a few related concepts and skills, so they can give all their attention to mastering those one or two items. The more children play, the more they will learn and improve. Some concepts and skills are repeated in two or more games. Play the ones you like the best.

The games

The games under each heading progress from the simplest to the more advanced. Many of the games have variations that can make the game different or more complex.

Under the title of each game, grade levels and correlating Common Core State Standards are listed for the game. Don't hesitate to try a game below your child's grade level. You might be surprised to discover that they need practice in the highlighted skill. And you can certainly try a game above your child's grade level. If it proves to be too difficult, change it or move on to a more suitable game.

Many of the games include some of my observations and comments. After playing these games countless times with hundreds of children, I've discovered that there were certain patterns of thinking and behaviors that almost always occurred. I share them here as one teacher to another and as one parent to another so you can benefit from what I've learned playing these games and to provide a starting point for your own observations.

Questions promote reflection and help children make mathematical connections. Good questioning involves responding to a child in a manner that helps them think and makes you aware of what they are thinking. Because this can be a challenge at first, I have included some questions in each game that I have often used that have proven to be effective.

Common Core State Standards

Professionals connected to the education of children are very aware of the Common Core State Standards, but if you're not a teacher or an administrator, they may be new to you. Educators and other experts developed the Common Core Standards based on research and lessons learned from top-performing countries. (The *Common Core State Standards for Mathematics* (NGA Center and CCSSO 2010) can be downloaded for printing at http://www.corestandards.org/assets /CCSSI_Math%20Standards.pdf.) The standards describe the skills and knowledge your children need to succeed in a rapidly changing world, including the ability to think creatively, solve real-world problems, make effective arguments, and engage in debates.

When it is appropriate, the number(s) of the exact standard(s) addressed by each game is indicated. If a game does not list a standard, that game was not designed to meet a specific standard at that grade level but developed to help children with mathematical concepts and skills that may need solidifying as well as with memory, visual discrimination, and critical thinking.

Helpful hints for playing the games

- It is very important that you use the correct mathematical language with children. Speaking and understanding the language of math is a central part of learning important concepts in math. Use the correct terms from the very beginning. You can connect the words to concepts or ideas that children are already familiar with. Talk about *sums* (the answer to an addition problem) or *differences* (the answer to a subtraction problem), and so on. In other words, talk the talk while you play the games. To help you do so, chapters requiring familiarity with specific math terms have a glossary.

- When playing games, children need to take responsibility for keeping each other accountable. I've found that the best way to accomplish this is to have players exchange papers and check each other's work. If a player has calculated correctly, the other player puts his or her initials by the calculation. If there is a mistake, it is not initialed, but given back to the player to correct the mistake, or you may have the children work together to resolve the error. Parents playing with their children can check each other's work, too. What fun it is when a child finds a miscalculation in their parent's work!

- Many games require counters. Anything will do—pennies, buttons, paper clips, pebbles, and such. I have found that the round transparent counters available at education supply stores work the very best. They allow the players to see what's under the counters.

- If you are making game cards, make sure to print them on a medium-color card stock or paper so that they cannot be read when facedown.

- Many other games allow the player who finds a pair to go again. This is not an effective strategy for keeping both players engaged. The games in this book don't allow for repeat turns. Make sure that players keep rotating turns.

- Once a game has been played and mastered, ask your children how that game might be changed or made more challenging, and then give it a try! Or go on to the variation or the next game.

Game resources and materials

Many of the games feature specific game boards, recording sheets, or cards. All these special materials are available as full-size black line masters on NCTM's More4U online resource center. Simply go to www.nctm.org/more4u and enter the access code that is on the first page of this book.

Playing cards

After working with children for many years, I developed a set of ten-frame cards that I think are far more helpful for playing card games with children than a standard deck of playing cards.

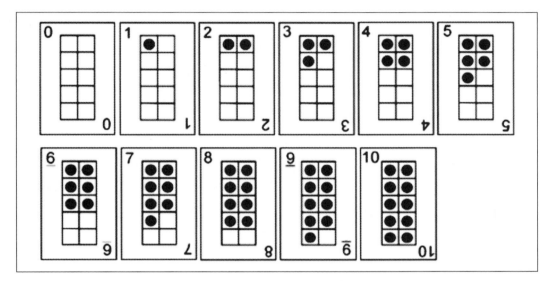

- These cards have a 0 (zero) and regular decks do not. Zero is a very important number concept in our base 10 system and should be included in most games. Turning a queen, for example, into a 0 is not helpful when playing number games with children.
- This deck has a 1 card. It is not always easy for children to visualize an ace as the number 1.
- The cards use a ten-frame, which shows a concrete representation of the amount each number represents; for example, a 7 has seven dots that are easily countable. It also anchors children to 10. The 7 shows seven dots and three blank spaces, so children can easily see and count how many more are needed to make 10.
- The cards are helpful in identifying odd and even numbers. If every dot has a partner, it is an even number. If one dot does not have a partner, it is an odd number.

The ten-frame deck of cards is like any other deck of cards in that there are four of each number in every deck.

Any standard deck of playing cards will be adequate, but I strongly recommend that you print and use the ten-frame cards on the National Council of Teachers of Mathematics More4U web page (www.nctm.org/more4u).

- Print the cards on a medium-dark card stock (I use salmon). Don't use white or any other really light colors. You don't want players to be able to see the numbers when the cards are facedown.

- Laminate them if possible. Most education supply stores have laminating machines. This really helps with longevity.
- Cut them apart and begin to play.

If you use a standard deck of playing cards, remove the face cards. None of the games need face cards.

Shuffling is very hard for children to do. It is all right to lay the cards facedown on a hard surface and mix them up. Making a neat pile might be a challenge for some children or it might take a good deal of time. Pushing the cards into a messy pile is completely acceptable. Players can choose a card from anywhere in the pile.

Dice

With young children, the bigger the dice, the better. The small dice used by adults make it hard to count the dots. If children have little experience with dice, they don't readily recognize the configurations, and may have to count the dots to know what number it represents. It won't take long before they roll a 6, for example, and know without counting the dots that it is a 6.

I also recommend that children use a big, heavy-duty paper plate for rolling dice. The paper plate softens the sound (most important in a classroom) and acts as a boundary for the dice. There are those eager-to-experiment children who want to roll the dice as far and as high as they can. The rule is that if a player rolls the die and it goes outside the plate, that player loses a turn.

Number Recognition and Counting

Introduction

Number Recognition and Counting to 10

Five 20

Cover Up! 21

Twins 23

Twins Concentration 24

Speed. 25

Number Recognition and Counting to 20

Fifteen 26

Exactly 20 27

Number Recognition and Counting to 30

Putting Pennies on a Plate 29

1 to 30 Bingo 31

Introduction

Children in kindergarten through second grade are expected to accurately and efficiently count sets of objects as well as produce sets of a given number. To do so, they need to develop a variety of counting skills and concepts.

Besides playing math games with their children, parents can support their children's mathematical growth at this age by counting things! Encourage your children to count all kinds of collections. Count marbles, silverware, Cheerios, paper clips, pebbles, stairs, French fries in your next fast food order, steps from the back door to the front door, cans in the pantry, furniture legs in the house, red cars on the road, buttons on clothes, things you have to plug in—anything!

Count collections by 1s, 2s, 5s, and 10s. Did the answer come out the same no matter how you counted it? This may seem obvious to adults, but to a child, it is a concept that needs to be learned.

These activities will provide children with rich opportunities to practice oral counting, develop more efficient counting strategies, group objects in strategic ways, and record numbers. The games will also give children chances to represent their thinking, which means they can talk about and use symbols or pictures to explain the mental methods they have used. This is important because adults can gain insight into what that child knows, understands, and is able to do.

Counting is one of the best ways to help children build number sense. Children need many experiences with counting to learn which number comes next, how this number sequence is related to the objects they are counting, and how to keep track of which ones have been counted and which still need to be counted.

Experience with counting provides a solid foundation for future experiences with addition, subtraction, multiplication, and division.

Five

The goal of the game is to be the first player to get the cards for 1 through 5 and to order them from smallest to greatest.

Number recognition and Sequencing to 5
Variation: Number recognition and Sequencing to 10
Kindergarten: CCSS.K.CC.C.7
Grade 1

Two players

Materials

- ten-frame cards 1–5, four of each,
  or the same if using a standard deck

How to play

The cards are shuffled and each player gets five cards. The remaining cards are placed facedown in a stack. The top card is turned over to create a discard pile.

Player 1 takes the top card from the facedown stack or discard pile, fitting it into her hand. Player 1 then discards one card.

Player 2 proceeds in the same manner.

Players alternate turns until one player has cards for 1 through 5. That player shows the other player his hand. The cards must be in order with 1 on the left and 5 on the right.

Questions

- What numbers don't you need because you already have them?

- What number(s) are you looking for?

- Would the number you need come before the _____ or after the_____?

- Is _____ less than_____ or more than _____?

Variation: The game is played in the same manner but the cards 1 to 10 are used and each player gets ten cards. The object of the game is to be the first player to get the cards 1 through 10 and to order them from the smallest to greatest

Cover Up!

The goal of this game is to be the first player to put a counter on all six numbers.

Number recognition to 6
Kindergarten

Variation 1: Number recognition to 10
Kindergarten: CCSS.K.CC.C.7
Grade 1

Variation 2: Addition to 12
Grade 1: CCSS.OA.C.6
Grade 2: CCSS.OA.B.2

Two players

Materials

- one die
- paper
- pencils
- six counters for each player
- 1–6 number line for each player

1	2	3	4	5	6

How to play

Player 1 rolls the die and puts a counter on that number on her number line.

Player 2 rolls the die and proceeds in the same manner.

If a player rolls a number that already has a counter on it, that player loses a turn.

The first player to cover 1 to 6 on the number line wins the game.

This game seems simple, but it helps young children recognize the dots on the die. When they begin, they may need to count the dots each time, but they will soon learn what number the dots represent without counting. The game also helps children learn to connect the counted number of dots to the numeral.

Variation 1: The game is the same but ten-frame cards 1 to 10, four of each, are used along with a 1 to 10 number line for each player.

1	2	3	4	5	6	7	8	9	10

Variation 2: In this variation, simple addition is required before placing a counter on a number. Two dice are rolled, and the numbers added. The counter is placed on the resulting sum. Each player uses a 1 to 12 number line.

1	2	3	4	5	6	7	8	9	10	11	12

After the children have played this game several times, ask them why no one was able to cover the 1 when using two dice. How can they solve that problem?

As children become proficient at playing Variation 2, have them record their rolls for each turn on a sheet of paper (see the sample below).

Turn 1	3 + 6 = 9
Turn 2	4 + 2 = 6
Turn 3	5 + 1 = 6
Turn 4	4 +5 = 9
Turn 5	1 + 1 = 2
Turn 6	6 + 6 = 12

Questions

- What are all the different number combinations you found that equaled the same sum? (For example, what different number combinations equaled 9 [3 + 6, 4 + 5, and so on]?)
- Were there any sums that had fewer possible combinations?

Twins

The goal of this game is to find as many "twins" (two 3s, for example) as possible.

Number recognition to 6
Variation: Number recognition to 10
Kindergarten
Grade 1

Two players

Materials

- ten-frame cards 0–6, four of each,
  or a standard deck 1–6, four of each

- one die

How to play

The cards are shuffled and placed facedown in a stack. Player 1 rolls the die and takes that number of cards from the facedown stack.

Example
Player 1 rolls a 4 and takes four cards from the stack.

If Player 1 has a set of twins, he lays the twins faceup and tells the other player what he has, for instance, "I have two sixes."

Player 2 proceeds in the same manner.

Players alternate turns until all the cards from the facedown stack are depleted.

The player with the most sets of twins is the winner.

Because number recognition is the goal of this game, children must verbalize the name of the number they are laying down. If you know that the child already knows the number names, then this is unnecessary.

Variation: The game is played in the same way, but ten-frame cards 0 to 10, four of each, are used.

Questions

- What numbers do you already have?

- What numbers do you need?

Twins Concentration

The goal of this game is to find like-numbered cards; for example, two 4s.

Number recognition to 10
Kindergarten
Grade 1
Grade 2

Two players

Materials

- ten-frame cards 0–10, two of each,
  or a standard deck 1–10, two of each

How to play

The cards are shuffled and placed facedown in a grid of four rows with five cards in each row and a last row of only two cards if using ten-frame cards.

Player 1 turns over any two cards, keeping them in place. If they are the same number, Player 1 tells Player 2 what the number is, for example, "I have two 4s," and then keeps the pair. If they are not the same number, Player 1 still verbalizes the numbers, but then turns the two cards back over.

Many games allow the player who finds a pair to immediately take another turn. I have discovered that this is not an effective strategy for keeping both players engaged. Make sure that players keep rotating turns.

Player 2 proceeds in the same manner.

Players alternate turns until no cards remain in the grid. Players then count their cards, and the player with the most cards wins.

Make sure that the cards stay in a fairly orderly grid. If the players turn over a card and leave it in exactly the same spot, it is easier to find a card that has been previously turned over. Children will often pick the card up as they turn it over and then put it back down in a different space. This leads to confusion.

Question

- You just turned over a _____. Where did you just see another _____?

Speed

The goal of the game is to sort the cards by number and order them from least to greatest.

Number recognition	**Sequencing numbers from 1 to 10**
Kindergarten	Kindergarten: CCSS.K.CC.C.7
	Grade 1
	Grade 2

One or more players

Materials

- deck of ten-frame cards for each player

How to play

The players shuffle their cards and place them faceup in a pile. The parent or teacher says go, and players sort their deck into piles according to number. When done, the stacks must be put into consecutive order from 1 on the left to 10 on the right.

The first player to sort all their cards correctly wins. All other players must complete the sorting and ordering of their cards.

Play this game over and over. Usually children begin by using very inefficient strategies. For instance, it is not uncommon for a child to spend a great deal of time hunting for all the 6s, then all the 2s, and so forth. As they continue to play, they begin to realize that there just might be a faster, more efficient way to accomplish the task. Encourage them to play this game with other children if possible. In observing the strategies of other children, they begin to notice and develop more efficient ways to sort.

Be careful not to tell them what to do. If they continue to use inefficient strategies to sort their cards, that's acceptable as long as they are gaining familiarity with the numbers and are able to sort them more quickly each time.

Questions

- Is there another way to sort the cards? Why don't you give it a try? Was it easier or faster?

Fifteen

This is a counting and strategy game. The goal of the game is to force the other player to take the last (fifteenth) counter.

Counting
Kindergarten
Grade 1
Grade 2

Two players

Materials

- fifteen counters

How to play

All the *counters* are placed between the two players. Players take turns removing only one, two, or three of the counters at a time.

Example
Player 1 chooses to take three counters. Player 2 chooses to take two.

The winner is the player who forces the other player to take the last (fifteenth) counter.

Variation 1: The game is played in the same manner, but the winner is the player who takes the last counter.

Variation 2: The object of the game remains the same, but any number of counters can be used.

This game encourages children to think ahead and develop strategies.

Questions

- Did you find any strategies that helped you win this game?
- Can you find a pattern you can use to make sure that you always win?

Exactly 20

The object of the game is to reach 20 *exactly*.

Number recognition and Counting
Kindergarten
Grade 1
Grade 2

Two players

Materials

- one die
- one game piece for each player
- 0–20 number line for each player

0	1	2	3	4	5	6	7	8	9	10	11	12	13	14	15	16	17	18	19	20

How to play

Each player puts his game piece on 0. Player 1 rolls the die and moves her game piece the number of spaces rolled, and says to the other player, "I landed on___." Player 2 rolls the die and proceeds in the same manner.

Players alternate turns.

If a player is getting close to 20 but cannot land exactly on 20, he or she must go back the number of spaces rolled on the die.

Example
Player 1 is on 18 and rolls a 4. Since a player must land on 20 to win, the 4 is too big a number, so instead of going forward, Player 1 must go back four spaces to 14.

Play continues until one player is able to land exactly on 20.

Because number recognition is one of the goals, it is important that children verbalize the number they have landed on each time they take a turn.

Questions

- As the children get closer to 20, here are some questions to ask:
- What do you need to roll to get to 20 exactly?

- Which numbers would be helpful but not get you all the way there?

- Which numbers would not be helpful because they would be too much?

- How likely is it that you will roll the ___ that you need?

Variation: Play the game until a player reaches 20 exactly; then reverse the goal to land exactly on 0.

Putting Pennies on the Plate

The goal of this game is to have the most pennies in the plate after five rolls of the die.

Number recognition and Counting to 30
Variation 1: Number recognition and Counting to 30
Variation 2: Number recognition and Counting to 60
Kindergarten: CCSS.K.CC.B.4a
CCSS.K.CC.B.5

Variation 3: Addition to 12	**Variation 4: Subtraction**
Kindergarten: CCSSK.OA.A.1	Kindergarten: CCSS.K.OA.A.1
Grade 1: CCSS.1.OA.C.6	Grade 1: CCSS.1.OA.A.1
Grade 2: CCSS.2.OA.B.2	Grade 2: CCSS.2.OA.B.2

Two players

Materials

- one die
- tub of pennies or other counters (at least 60)
- paper plate for each player
- pencils

How to play

Player 1 rolls the die, takes that number of pennies from the tub, and puts them on her plate. Player 2 checks to make sure Player 1 has counted correctly, and then rolls the die. Play proceeds in the same manner.

Players alternate turns until all players have had five turns. They then count their pennies. The player who has the most pennies is the winner.

It's important that children learn to count collections, such as the pennies, in different ways. Count them by ones, twos, threes, fives, and tens. Young children may not realize that the total should be the same no matter how it is counted. Ask them if the total number of pennies was the same or different when counted in particular ways. Many experiences with counting all kinds of things will lead children to the correct conclusion.

Questions

- If your goal is to have the greatest amount of pennies, which numbers do you want to roll?
- Will the same be true if you want the least amount of pennies?

Variation 1: The game is played in the same manner, but the winner is the player with the least number of pennies.

Variation 2: The game is the same, but each player takes ten turns.

Variation: 3 The object of the game is the same, but simple addition is required before taking any pennies. Two dice are used, and the numbers added together. The player takes the resulting sum of pennies.

With first and second graders, you might wish to have them record the equations generated by their turns on a sheet of paper.

Turn 1	$2 + 4 = 6$
Turn 2	$6 + 3 = 9$
Turn 3	$2 + 1 = 3$
Turn 4	$5 + 2 = 7$
Turn 5	$1 + 4 = 5$

Variation 4: This game introduces the concept of subtraction with its goal of getting to 0 by taking pennies from the plate. Fifty (or any number chosen) pennies are placed on a plate. Players roll the die and remove (subtract) pennies from the plate. The first player to take away all the pennies, reaching 0, is the winner.

As you use this variation, be sure to use the words *subtract* and *take away* interchangeably. This will begin to cement an important mathematical term and its meaning in children's minds. Get to the point where *subtract* is the only word you use.

1 to 30 Bingo

The goal of this game is to get four counters in a vertical, horizontal, or diagonal row.

Number recognition
Kindergarten
Grade 1
Sequencing numbers from 1 to 10
Kindergarten: CCSS.K.CC.C.7
Grade 1
Grade 2

Two players

Materials

- counters for each player
- 1 to 30 Bingo game board for each player
- number cards for teacher or parent
  (Cut apart one bingo board for cards.)

13	2	7	25	18
9	22	15	4	30
19	6	24	17	10
1	20	27	8	16
12	3	26	14	29
5	11	21	28	23

This game is intended to be noncompetitive, so only one bingo board is needed. Allow the children to work together to find particular numbers. You will quickly discover which children need to play this game more than once.

How to play

The teacher or parent shuffles the cards and pulls one out. She calls out the number and holds the card up so it can be seen.

Players cover the number called with a counter. The first player to get four in a vertical, horizontal, or diagonal row wins the game.

Keep in mind that some young children have a hard time recognizing a row that is made diagonally.

Questions

- Looking at the numbers you already have covered, what numbers are you hoping get called?
- What numbers would not be particularly helpful?

Comparing Numbers to 10

Introduction

Activities

Greater Than/Less Than Paper Plates 34

Three Symbols 34

Number Line Challenge 35

Comparing Numbers to 6

I Have the Greatest! 36

Beat the Die 38

Comparing Numbers to 10

More or Less... 39

GLEE.. 41

Close to 5 43

In Between 44

Salute 46

Introduction

It is helpful to know if one number is greater than, less than, or equal to another number.

In life, comparing numbers is an important skill. Will you buy the $1.69 can of tomatoes or the $.99 can of tomatoes? What's the difference between a house with 900 square feet and a house with 1,249 square feet? Does this recipe need 1/4 cup sugar or 1/2 cup? Daily life is full of comparisons.

Children do not automatically know if a number is greater than or less than another number as adults do. They are still forming a way of visualizing these relationships mentally, and will need plenty of exposure to the numbers before that happens.

When children compare numbers, they develop number sense and build number relationships.

Children begin to compare numbers in kindergarten by using the words *greater than, less than*, and *equal to*. They should be able to mentally compare numbers up to 10 in their head or by counting on their fingers.

In math we use three important symbols for these ideas:

- greater than (>); 8 is greater than 4, 8 > 4

- less than (<); 4 is less than 8, 4 < 8

- equals sign (=); 5 is equal to 5, 5 = 5

The concept of equal is very important in math. It means that both sides of the equals symbol (=) have the same value. The values are balanced, or equal.

The two symbols for greater than (>) and less than (<) can be easily confused. It can be hard to remember which is for the larger number, and which is for the smaller.

The open parts of the symbols always face the *greater number*. The smaller, pointy ends of the symbols always face the *smaller number*. Many teachers have successfully recast the symbols as the mouth of a hungry alligator that always wants to eat the bigger number.

Try the following activities before playing the games in this section. They will introduce, reinforce, and help the children visualize the concepts behind the three symbols.

Activities

Greater Than/Less Than Paper Plates

If children are struggling with the concepts of greater than and less than, take out two paper plates and place an unequal number of objects on each plate. Ask the child to count the objects on each plate; then ask, "Which plate has the greater number than the other?" In math, "greater" usually means "more." Which plate has "less" or "fewer"?

Three Symbols

Materials

- two paper plates
- one piece of paper with an open triangle (>)
- one piece of paper with an equals sign (=)

How to play

Put the two paper plates side by side. Place unequal or equal amounts of counters on each plate.

Have the children count them, write the number of objects on each plate, and then insert one of the signs between the two paper plates.

Repeat with different numbers.

Begin to have the children "read" what they are seeing, for instance, "Seven is greater than four." Ask them for another way that can be stated, such as "Four is less than seven."

Comparing numbers will be needed later on when children will have to—
- compare higher numbers, like 67 and 76;
- use a number line to solve other types of problems; and
- identify "1 more than 45," "10 less than 97," and so on.

Number Line Challenge

A number line helps some children visualize *greater than* and *less than* in a linear fashion.

0	1	2	3	4	5	6	7	8	9	10

Materials

- 0–10 number line
- 0–20 number line
- hundred board

more**4**U

How to play

Have your child point to a number on the line. Which numbers are greater than that number (that is, come after the number)? Which numbers are less than the number (come before the number)?

Number lines are also helpful as children begin to compare larger numbers from 11 to 20 and up. Hundred charts are useful, too.

0	1	2	3	4	5	6	7	8	9	10	11	12	13	14	15	16	17	18	19	20

I Have the Greatest!

The goal of the game is to have the greatest number of counters after ten rolls of the die.

Comparing numbers to 6
Variation 1: Comparing numbers to 6
Kindergarten: CCSS.K.CC.C.7
Grade 1
Grade 2

Variation 2: Comparing numbers to 10
Kindergarten: CCSS.K.CC.C.7
Grade 1
Grade 2

Variation 3: Addition to 12
Grade 1: CCSS.1.OA.C.6
Grade 2: CCSS.2.OA.B.2

Two players

Materials

- two dice, one for each player
- counters
- "I Have the Greatest!" recording sheet

Round	Player Name	< > =	Player Name
1			
2			
3			
4			
5			
6			
7			
8			
9			
10			

How to play

Players roll their dies at the same time. The player with the greater number takes a counter and says, "___ is greater than ___, I get a counter."

If the players roll the same number, they both get a counter. At the end of ten turns, the player with more counters is the winner.

At varying points in the game, stop the play and say, "Convince me that ____ is greater than ____," or "Prove to me that ____ is less than ____."

When the children can readily determine *greater than*, *less than*, and *equal to*, have them record what happened each time using the symbols on their recording sheets.

Round	Player Name	< > =	Player Name
Sample	5	>	2
Sample	1	<	3
Sample	4	=	4

Variation 1: The game is played in the same way, but the player with the lesser number takes a counter and says, " ___ is less than ___."

Variation 2: Instead of rolling dice, the game is played using ten-frame cards 0 to 10 or a standard deck 1 to 10.

Variation 3: "I Have the Greatest Sum!" is played in the same way, but each player rolls two dice and adds the numbers together. Then the players decide who has the greater than and less than sum or if their sums are equal. The sums and appropriate symbols are recorded in a grid. (A sample sheet is below.)

Turns	Player Name	< > =	Player Name
Sample	5 + 3 = 8	>	2 + 4 = 6
Sample	1 + 1 = 2	<	3 + 6 = 9
Sample	4 + 2 = 6	=	1 + 5 = 6

Beat the Die

The goal of the game is to take a card that is equal to or greater than the number on the die.

Comparing numbers to 6
Kindergarten: CCSS.K.CC.C.7
Grade 1
Grade 2

Two players

Materials

- one die
- ten-frame cards 1–6, four of each,
  or the same if using a standard deck

How to play

The cards are shuffled and divided equally between the players. Players put their cards facedown in a pile.

Player 1 rolls the die, and both players turn over one card from their pile. The player who has the card *equal to* or *greater than* the number on the die takes both cards. If both players turned over a card that is *less than* the roll of the die, the die is rolled again.

In the event that both players have numbers that are greater than the die, the player with the greatest number takes both cards. If there is a tie, each player turns over one more card and lays it on top of the first card. The player with the greater number on this top card takes all four cards.

Players alternate turns rolling the die until all of the cards have been used. Players count their cards; the winner is the player with the most cards.

Questions

Ask these questions *after* the die has been rolled but *before* each player turns over a card:

- What numbers are you hoping you will turn over?
- Would anything else be helpful?
- What numbers would not be helpful?

More or Less

You may know this game as "War." For mathematical purposes, it is more appropriate to call it "More or Less." The goal of this game is to draw a card whose number is greater than the other player's.

Comparing numbers to 10

Variation 1: Comparing numbers to 10	**Variation 2: Addition to 20**
Kindergarten: CCSS.K.CC.C.7	Grade 1: CCSS.1.OA.C.6
Grade 1	Grade 2: CCSS.2.OA.B.2
Grade 2	

Two players

Materials

- 0–10 number line
- ten-frame cards

How to play

The cards are shuffled and divided equally between the players. Players put their cards facedown in a pile.

The players turn over their top card at the same time. The player with the greater number ("more"), says, "_____ is greater than _____," and collects both cards.

In the event that both players turn over the same number, players turn over one more card and put it on top of their first card. The player with the greater number on this top card verbalizes the "greater than" statement and takes all four cards.

Play continues until all the cards in the facedown piles have been used; players then count the cards they have accumulated during the game. The player with more cards wins the game.

Make sure that children verbalize their numbers when they are comparing two numbers. Using the correct mathematical language—greater than, less than, equal to—is important.

Many young children may have to count and compare the dots on each card to determine whether a number is greater than or less than another number. After playing the games enough times, they will begin to *know* without counting whether a number is greater than or less than another number. Many times a 0 to 10 number line is a useful tool that helps children visualize greater than and less than numbers.

0	1	2	3	4	5	6	7	8	9	10

Variation 1: "Less" is played in a similar manner, but the player with the number that is "less" collects the cards.

Variation 2: The game is played in a similar manner, but each player turns over two cards and adds them together. The player with "more" or "less" (depending on which game is being played) verbalizes their statement. For example, "I have six plus six equals twelve and that is more than the five plus two equals seven that you have," or "I have three plus five equals eight and that is less than the five plus six equals eleven that you have."

Questions

- Convince me that _____ is less than _____.
- If you turn over a _____, what numbers would be more? What numbers would be less?
- Prove that three plus three is more than one plus two.

GLEE

(Greater Than, Less Than, and Equal To Exercise)

The goal of GLEE is to have the second number be greater than the first number.

Comparing numbers to 10
Kindergarten: CCSS.K.CC.C.7
Grade 1
Grade 2

Two players

Materials

- ten-frame cards 0–10, two of each,
  or a standard deck 1–10, two of each

How to play

The cards are shuffled and placed facedown in a grid of four rows with five cards in each row with a fifth row of only two cards if using ten-frame cards.

Player 1 turns over one card and tells Player 2 what that number is. Then Player 1 turns over a second card and tells Player 2 what that second number is. If the second card is greater than the first card, Player 1 says, "_____ is greater than _____," and keeps both cards. If the second card is less than the first card, Player 1 says, "_____ is less than _____," and turns both cards facedown, keeping the cards in place.

Example
Player 1 turns over a 5, and says to Player 2, "It is a five." He then turns over his second card, an 8, and tells Player 2, "It is an eight." Because eight is greater than five, Player 1 verbalizes "Eight is greater than five" and keeps both cards.

If a player turns over two cards that are the same, the player says, "_____ and _____ are equal." Because both numbers are equal, they are not greater than each other, so they are turned back over.

Player 2 proceeds in the same manner.

Players alternate turns until all the cards from the grid are used. They then count their cards. The player with the most cards is the winner and must say to the other player, for example, "I have twelve cards, and you have ten cards. Twelve is greater than ten."

Make sure that the children verbalize their numbers when comparing two numbers. Using the correct mathematical language (greater than, less than, and equal to) is important.

Many young children may have to count and compare the dots on each card to determine whether a number is greater than or less than another number. After playing the games enough times, they will begin to know without counting whether a number is greater than or less than another number. Many times a 0 to 10 number line is a useful tool that helps children visualize greater than, less than, and equal to.

0	1	2	3	4	5	6	7	8	9	10

As the children gain proficiency in the game, they should record each turn using the greater than, less than, and equals symbols on a sheet of paper (see the following sample).

Turn 1	8 > 5
Turn 2	1 < 4

Questions

After a player has turned over the first card, ask the following:

- What numbers are you hoping to turn over because they are greater than your first number?

- What numbers will not be helpful because they are less than your first number?

Variation: "Less Than" is played exactly the same way as "GLEE" except that players can take both cards only if their second card is less than their first card.

Close to 5

The goal of this game is to draw a number that is closer to 5 than the other player's number.

Comparing numbers to 10
Kindergarten: CCSS.K.CC.C.7
Grade 1
Grade 2

Two players

Materials

- ten-frame cards
- 0–10 number line for each player

0	1	2	3	4	5	6	7	8	9	10

How to play

The cards are shuffled and placed facedown in a stack. Each player takes one card. The player with the card closest to 5 wins both cards.

Example
Player 1 draws a 2. Player 2 draws a 7. Player 2 takes both cards because 7 is closer to 5 than 2 is.

If both players have numbers that are an equal distance from 5, both players lay another card on top of their first card. The player whose number is closer to 5 on this last card takes all four cards.

Play continues until the facedown stack of cards is gone. Players count their cards; the player with more cards wins the game.

Questions

- Is your card greater than 5 or less than 5?
- How far from 5 is your card?
- What numbers lie between your number and 5?
- How do you know your number is closer to 5 than the other player's?
- How far from 5 is the other player's number?

In Between

The object of this game is to have the fifth number drawn fall between the spread of a player's first two numbers.

Comparing numbers to 10
Kindergarten: CCSS.K.CC.C.7
Grade 1
Grade 2

Two players

Materials

- ten-frame cards
- paper
- pencils

How to play

The cards are shuffled and placed facedown in a stack.

Each player takes two cards from the stack and arranges them with the smaller number on the left and the greater number on the right. One player turns over a fifth card. Players score a point if this fifth number falls between the two they already have.

Example
Player 1 turns over 2 and 5. Player 2 turns over 4 and 6. The fifth card turned over is a 3. Player 1 scores a point because 3 comes between 2 and 5. Player 2 does not score a point because 3 does not come between 4 and 6.

The five cards are put in a discard pile, and each player selects two new cards and arranges them smaller to greater. Again, a fifth card is turned over for comparison.

Play continues until a player gets twenty points.

For some children, a 0 to 10 number line might be helpful.

0	1	2	3	4	5	6	7	8	9	10

They can lay their cards on the number line and have a concrete way to see which numbers come between their two numbers.

Some children will be confused when they draw two consecutive numbers, such as 5 and 6. They will ask if a 7 falls between 5 and 6. Here's where the number line will help.

Questions

After both players have their numbers in place from smaller to greater, ask them:

- When the fifth card is turned over, what numbers do you hope to see?

- What numbers wouldn't be helpful to you? Why?

Salute

The goal of this game is to figure out the unknown number, the "salute" number, by asking the other players three questions.

Comparing numbers to 10
Kindergarten: CCSS.K.CC.C.7
Grade 1
Grade 2

Two to six players

Materials

- ten-frame cards

How to play

Players should be seated in a circle facing each other. The cards are shuffled and placed facedown in a stack.

Player 1 picks up one card and, *without looking at it*, holds it on his forehead so that everyone else can see it. No one should tell him what the number is. It's his job to figure out the number by asking the other players questions.

Player 1, holding the card on his forehead, asks Player 2, "Is it a ____?" Player 2 responds using the words *less than*, *greater than*, or *equal to*. Player 1 asks other players questions, and then tries to figure out the exact number of his card.

Example
Player 1 puts a 4 on his forehead. He doesn't know what the number is, but everyone else does.

Player 1 asks Player 2, "Is it a nine?" Player 2 responds, "Less than nine."

Player 1 asks Player 3, "Is it a two?" Player 3 responds, "More than two."

Player 1 asks another player, "Is it a four?" The other player responds, "It is equal to four."

If he guesses the number on his card after three questions, he may keep the card. If he doesn't guess the number after three questions, he must keep guessing until he knows the number, but he does not get to keep the card. It is returned to the bottom of the stack.

Players take turns drawing a number and asking questions.

Play continues for a set time. The player with the most cards at the end of the game is the winner.

I love this game, and as children learn it and become more confident, they love it, too. While there is no time limit to this game, be alert to waning interest on the part of the children. Depending on the number of players (four to six is optimal) and how quickly the "salute" numbers are solved, fifteen to thirty minutes of play usually keeps the children engaged. Be aware, there are always some children who just can't resist peeking as they pick up a card and put it on their forehead!

Until they learn the number sequence from 0 to 10 really well, this game may be hard for some children. Some may need a 0 to 10 number line to visualize what the other children are telling them. I often use a number line along with two movable arrows that are "greater than" or "less than" symbols.

0	1	2	3	**4<**	5	6	7	8	**<9**	10

Is it a 9? It's less than 9. Is it a 4? It's greater than 4. Now the child should be able to see that the number on her forehead is between 4 and 9.

If children struggle with this, use cards 0 to 5 and a 0 to 5 number line.

Questions

- If it's greater than ____, what numbers could it be? What numbers won't it be?
- If it's less than ____, what numbers could it be? What numbers won't it be?

The Games

Addition

Introduction

Glossary 51

Adding One More

What's One More? 52

One More 54

Adding to 10

What Equals 5? 56

Find 6 58

Addends Hunt 59

Target Addition 61

Addition War 62

Addition Ladder 63

Gone! 65

Pyramid 67

What Does It Take to Get to 10? 69

Addition Concentration 71

Rummy to 10 73

Same Sum 74

Adding to 20

Can You Find 11? 76

Searching for Sums 77

A Colorful Quilt 78

The Three Dice Game 80

Four-in-a-Row—Sums to 18 82

Three Strikes 84

Addition

Get Close to 20 85

The Constant Addend 87

Stop! 88

Adding Doubles 90

Salute Addition 92

Balancing Both Sides 94

Addition to 30

21 96

Reach 25 97

Set It Aside 99

Estimates or Smart Guesses 101

Introduction

The National Council of Teachers of Mathematics (NCTM) maintains that because subtraction is the inverse operation of addition, it is necessary to teach both processes at the same time. This helps children understand how addition and subtraction are related. *I completely agree.* However, for the purpose of this book, they are treated in two separate chapters.

The Common Core State Standards for Mathematics (NGA Center and CCSSO 2010) states, "By end of Grade 2, [children should] know from memory all sums of two one-digit numbers (p. 19)." I like to include ten with that.

Examples
What equals 10? 10 + 0, 9 + 1, 8 + 2, 7 + 3, 6 + 4, 5 + 5, 4 + 6, 3 + 7, 2 + 8, 1 + 9, 0 + 10
What equals 9? 9 + 0, 8 + 1, 7 + 2, 6 + 3, 5 + 4, 5 + 5, 3 + 6, 2 + 7, 1 + 8, 0 + 9

By the end of second grade, all of these one-digit addition facts need to be in long-term memory to be instantly recalled as needed. Once they are fixed in long-term memory, subtraction will be easier. In other words, a child needs to *know and understand* that 7 + 3 = 10 before they will really understand that 10 – 7 = 3.

Many children will use their fingers to count. This is a very useful strategy for young children to use to find any sum. To use 2 + 3 = 5 as an example, they will begin by putting up two fingers on one hand and three fingers on the other, and then count the fingers on both hands.

At some point, children will pick one of the numbers (it doesn't matter which one) and keep it "in their head" and count out the other; for instance, 2 is fixed in the mind and 3 is counted "3, 4, 5" on three fingers of one hand. Then they will begin to fix the bigger number in memory and count out the smaller number. Both of these stages arrive at different times for different children. For the most part, children can't be hurried into them.

The dots on the ten-frame cards are enormously helpful to children who need to count for addition. It is strongly recommended that they be printed out on a medium-dark card stock, laminated for longevity (if possible), and cut out to form a "deck." A deck consists of four of each number.

Children usually need to practice any addition fact *at least* 200 times before it goes into long-term memory and can be instantly recalled. The following addition games provide enough active repetition so that the facts are more easily (and happily) learned.

I have worked with many fifth- and sixth-grade students who resort to counting on their fingers because they do not have these facts in instant recall. Their success in math is hampered. Fluency with small numbers is critical to proficiency with large numbers.

Play a variety of the following addition games. They are sequenced from easy to the more complex. Don't assume that the first games are too easy for your children. Give the games a try. If they are too easy, go on to one of the game's variations or to the next game.

Addition Glossary

When playing any math game, it is important that the children become familiar with the correct math terminology for certain facts and concepts. In this section there are four words that should be introduced and consistently used; their definitions are below.

Addend is any number added to another to get a sum or total.

Sum is the total (whole amount) realized as a result of adding numbers (addends).

Equal is having the same amount or identical value.

Equation, sometimes called a number sentence, is a mathematical statement containing an equals sign that shows that two expressions are equal in value.

addend		addend	equals sign	sum		
3	+	7	=	10		

addend		addend	equals sign	addend		addend
4	+	3	=	5	+	2

What's One More?

The goal of the game is to have four counters in a vertical, horizontal, or diagonal row.

Addition
Variation: Adding 2
Kindergarten: CCSS.K.OA.A.5
Grade 1: CSS.1.OA.C.6
Grade 2

Two players

Materials

- die
- counters
- "What's One More?" game board for each player

more**4**U

2	3	4	5	6	7
3	4	5	6	7	2
4	5	6	7	2	3
5	6	7	2	3	4
6	7	2	3	4	5
7	2	3	4	5	6

How to play

Player 1 rolls the die and places a counter on one of the numbers that is "one more" than the number rolled. He verbalizes the rolled number and the "one more" number to Player 2. Player 2 rolls the die and proceeds in the same manner.

Example
Player 1 rolls a 4 and puts a counter on one of the 5s. He says, "I rolled a four, and one more than four is five." Player 2 rolls a 3 and puts a counter on one of the 4s. She says, "I rolled a three, and one more than three is four."

Players alternate turns. A player who cannot place a counter after rolling the die loses the turn.

The winner is the player who gets four counters in a vertical, horizontal, or diagonal row.

A 0 to 10 number line might be helpful so that children can visualize what they are being asked to do.

0	1	2	3	4	5	6	7	8	9	10

Questions

- What numbers are you hoping to roll? Why?
- Why did you put your counter on that particular _____ and not another _____ ?

Variation: "What's Two More?" is played in a similar fashion, using the game board below to play.

3	4	5	6	7	8
4	5	6	7	8	3
5	6	7	8	3	4
6	7	8	3	4	5
7	8	3	4	5	6
8	3	4	5	6	7

One More

The object of this game is to find two cards where one card's number is "one more" than the other number.

Addition: Adding 1
Variations: Adding 2 or 3 or more
Kindergarten: CCSS.K.OA.A.5
Grade 1: CCSS.1.OA.C.6
Grade 2: CCSS.2.OA.B.2

Two players

Materials

- ten-frame cards

How to play

Players sit side by side. Shuffle cards and place facedown in a stack.

Player 1 takes ten cards and places them faceup in a line in front of both players. She looks for two cards where one number is one more than the other number. When Player 1 selects correctly, she says, "I can take these cards because _____ is one more than _____."

Example
Player 1 picks a 7 and a 6, and says, "I can take these cards because seven is one more than six."

Player 2 adds two cards from the facedown stack to the faceup line, keeping ten cards in the line, and then proceeds in the same manner. (Note: Players always add two cards to the faceup line from the facedown stack at the beginning of their turn so it always has ten cards.)

If there are no cards in the line with a number that is one more than another, another card is added to the line for a total of eleven cards.

Players alternate turns until the facedown pile is gone and all possible one-more-number card pairs in the faceup line have been made.

The game can simply end here, or the players can count their cards, and the player with the most cards wins the game.

A 0 to 10 number line might be helpful so that children can visualize what they are being asked to do.

0	1	2	3	4	5	6	7	8	9	10

Questions

- The first number that you picked up is a _____. What number are you looking for that is one more than a _____?

- Can you prove to me that _____ is one more than _____?

Variations: Play the game the same way, but increase the "more" increments to two, three, and so on. A 0 to 20 number line might be helpful so that children can visualize what they are being asked to do.

0	1	2	3	4	5	6	7	8	9	10	11	12	13	14	15	16	17	18	19	20

What Equals 5?

The object of this Concentration-type game is to find two addends whose sum equals 5.

Addition to 10
Kindergarten

Variations: Addition to 12 and on
Grade 1: CCSS.1.OA.C.6
Grade 2: CCSS.2.OA.B.2

Two players

Materials

- ten–frame cards 0–5, two of each,
  or a standard deck 1–4, two of each

Pregame practice

The practice game with the cards *faceup* allows the children to visually see what they are expected to do mathematically.

The cards are shuffled and placed faceup in a grid of three rows with four cards in each row (or a grid of two rows with four cards if using a standard deck of cards).

Players take turns finding two addends (cards) whose sum equals five. As they find them, they take the two cards off the grid.

How to play

The cards are shuffled and placed facedown in a grid of three rows with four cards in each row (or a grid of two rows with four cards if using a standard deck of cards).

Player 1 turns over two cards, leaving them in place, and adds the numbers together. Player 1 verbalizes the equation whether or not it equals five; for example, "Five plus two equals seven." Since those two cards do not equal five, Player 1 turns them back over.

Player 2 turns over two cards, leaving them in place, and adds them together. Player 2 verbalizes the equation, for instance, "Zero plus five equals five." Because the sum of these two addends equals five, Player 2 takes the cards off the grid and puts them in a stack to her side.

Many games allow the player who finds a pair to go again. I have discovered that this is not an effective strategy for keeping both players engaged. Make sure that players keep alternating turns.

Players alternate turns until all the matches have been made. The players count their cards, and the one with the most cards wins the game.

When first playing this game, some children may need to count the dots on the cards to know what the two numbers equal. This is perfectly normal. The more they play, the more frequently you will see that they no longer need to count the dots. They are beginning to put those simple facts, for example, 4 + 1 = 5, in long-term memory.

Questions

• You just turned over a _____. What would you add to _____ to equal 5?

• What can you do to figure it out?

• Prove to me that _____ plus _____ equals 5.

Variations: Using the same game format, you can use two of each ten-frame cards 0 to 6, 0 to 7, and on to 0 to 10, looking for pairs of cards whose sums equal 6, 7, 8, 9, or 10. Be sure to adjust the grid to accommodate the greater number of cards.

Find 6

This is a solitaire game. The goal of the game is to find addends that equal 6.

Addition to 6
Kindergarten: CCSS.K.OA.A.5

Variations: Addition to 10
Grade 1: CCSS.1.OA.C.6
Grade 2: CCSS.2.OA.B.2

One player

Materials

- ten-frame cards 0–6, four of each,
  or a standard deck 1–5, four of each

How to play

The cards are shuffled and placed facedown in a stack. The top twelve cards are placed *faceup* in a grid of three rows with four cards in each row.

The player looks for combinations of two (or more) addends (cards) that equal 6. Once the player finds a combination, he takes those addends off the grid and adds new cards from the facedown stack to fill the gaps in the grid.

If none of the addends in the grid add up to 6, add another row of four cards to the bottom of the grid. Play continues until no more combinations of 6 can be made.

Variations: Once children have become really good at finding combinations adding up to 6, add the four 7s to the game and find combinations that equal 7. You will need the top sixteen cards to make a faceup grid of four rows with four cards in each row. As the children become proficient at finding the combinations for each sum, add the 8s, 9s, and 10s, tacking on a row to the grid each time.

Questions

- What are you looking for to go with this _____ that will equal 6?
- Is there another combination of addends that will equal 6?

Children may have to count the dots to know if two cards equal six. This is an early strategy that children will leave behind as the facts are committed to memory. You will see this happening when you ask what they are looking for to go with that 3 card, and they immediately say three.

It is important to note when a child realizes that three numbers can equal six, for example, $2 + 3 + 1 = 6$. Oftentimes children will ask if this is "OK." My response is, "Does it equal six? Isn't the name of this game "Find 6"?

I never point out to children that there are three numbers on the board that equal 6. I want them to think and see it for themselves, and then share what they have discovered with the other players.

Addends Hunt

The goal of this game is to color five boxes in a vertical, horizontall or diagonal row.

Addition to 9
Kindergarten
Grade 1: CCSS.1.OA.C.6
Grade 2: CCSS.2.OA.B.2

Two players

Materials

- ten-frame cards 4–9, four of each; the same if using a standard deck

- one crayon for each player

- "Addends Hunt" game board for each player

1	3	4	6	1	6
8	2	2	3	2	4
3	3	2	4	4	5
1	4	5	2	3	1
7	5	2	6	1	3
1	3	7	2	5	4

How to play

The cards are shuffled and placed facedown in a stack. Player 1 draws a card and colors in two adjacent addends on the game board whose sum equals the number on his card. The addends must be side by side or one above the other—no diagonals. Player 1 puts the card in a discard pile.

Example
Player 1 draws a 5. He may color 4 and 1 or 3 and 2.

1	3	4	6	1	6
8	2	2	3	2	4
3	3	2	4	4	5
1	4	5	2	3	1
7	5	2	6	1	3
1	3	7	2	5	4

Player 2 draws a card and proceeds in the same manner.

Players alternate turns. If a player draws a card and cannot find two adjacent addends to color, that player loses his turn.

Play continues until one player colors five addends in a vertical, horizontal, or diagonal row.

Questions

- You just drew a _____. What two numbers could you add together to equal _____? Can you think of any other numbers that equal _____?

- Looking at your game board, what sum are you hoping to draw? How likely are you to pick that sum?

Target Addition

The object of this game is to find two addends that equal the target sum.

Addition to 10
Kindergarten
Grade 1: CCSS.1.OA.C.6
Grade 2: CCSS.2.OA.B.2

Two players

Materials

- ten-frame cards
- target sum board

Target Sum

How to play

The cards are shuffled and placed in a facedown stack. Player 1 draws the top card and places it faceup on the target-sum board. This is the target sum. If a 0 is drawn for the target sum, the card is placed at the bottom of the stack and another card is drawn.

All the remaining cards are placed faceup around the target sum so the numbers can be seen.

Player 2 looks for two cards with addends that when added together will equal the target sum.

Example
Player 1 turns over a 6; it is the target sum. Player 2 looks for two cards whose addends equal 6, for example, 2 + 4, 5 + 1, 3 + 3, or 0 + 6.

Player 1 then looks for two cards with addends that equal the target sum.

Players alternate turns, continuing to look for two cards whose addends equal the target sum. When no more combinations can be found, the cards are reshuffled and Player 2 draws a different target sum.

Questions

- How do you know that you have found all the combinations that equal _____?
- What are all the combinations that equal the target sum?
- Could there be three addends that when added together equal the target sum?

Addition War

The object of the game is to draw two addends cards whose sum is greater than the sum of the two addends of the other player.

Addition to 10
Variation 1: Addition to 15 with three addends
Kindergarten
Grade 1: CCSS.1.OA.C.6
Grade 2: CCSS.2.OA.B.2

Variation 2: Addition to 20
Grade 1: CCSS.1.OA.C.6
Grade 2: CCSS.2.OA.B.2

Two players

Materials

- ten-frame cards 0–5, four of each, or a standard deck 1–5, four of each

How to play

The cards are shuffled and divided evenly between the two players. Players put their cards facedown in a stack.

Players turn over the top two cards on their stack and add the addends. They verbalize their equations to each other; for example, "Four plus three equals seven." Make sure the players give the entire equation, not just the sum.

The player whose addends add up to the greater sum gets all four of the cards.

In the event each player has the same sum, players turn over one more card and add the addend to their total. The greater sum wins all six cards.

Play continues until all the cards in the facedown stacks have been used. Players count their cards, and the player with more accumulated cards is the winner.

Questions

- Prove to me that you have the greater sum.
- What two addends would you need to have a sum greater than the other player?
- How is it that you have the same sums, but you have different addends?

Variation 1: The game is played in the same way, but each player turns over three cards and finds the sum. In the event of a tie, each player takes a fourth card and adds that addend to her total.

Variation 2: The entire deck of ten-frame cards 0 to 10 is used to play the game.

Addition Ladder

The goal of this game is to create addition equations that allow a player to put an equation on all the rungs of the "ladder."

Addition to 10
Kindergarten
Grade 1: CCSS.1.OA.C.6
Grade 2: CCSS.2.OA.B.2

Two or more players

Materials

- ten-frame cards
- pencils
- "Addition Ladder" recording sheet for each player

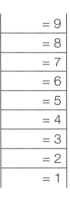

How to play

The cards are shuffled and placed facedown in a stack.

Player 1 takes five cards and puts them faceup in a line. He uses two of the cards to make an equation that has a sum of 1 to 9 and writes that equation on his ladder on the appropriate rung. Player 1 then discards the two used cards.

Example

Player 1 has cards 7, 9, 1, 4, and 3. He makes the equation 4 + 3 = 7 and writes it on the 7 rung of his ladder.

	= 9
	= 8
4 + 3 = 7	
	= 6
	= 5
	= 4
	= 3
	= 2
	= 1

Player 2 takes five cards from the stack and proceeds in the same manner.

Before each subsequent turn, players draw two more cards from the facedown stack so that they always have five cards to work with.

Players can put only one equation on each line. If a player cannot use her cards to place an equation on an empty line, she picks two cards from her faceup cards to put in the discard pile and loses her turn.

If players run out of cards in the facedown stack, they reshuffle the discard pile, stack it facedown, and continue to play.

Players alternate turns until one player wins by filling in all nine rungs on his ladder.

Questions

- What did you discover while playing this game?
- Where there any sums that were more difficult to make? Why?
- What equations could you use that would equal _____?
- What's a strategy you might try for the next game?

Gone!

The goal of this game is to cross off all the sums on the number line.

Addition to 10
Kindergarten
Grade 1: CCSS.1.OA.C.6
Grade 2: CCSS.2.OA.B.2

Two players

Materials

- ten-frame cards 0–5, four of each
- one crayon for each player
- 0–10 number line for each player

0	1	2	3	4	5	6	7	8	9	10

How to play

The cards are shuffled and placed facedown in a stack.

Player 1 takes two cards and finds the sum of those two addends. She colors that sum on her 0 to 10 number line and discards the two cards.

Example
Player 1 takes a 2 and a 5, and colors the 7 on her number line.

Player 2 takes two cards and proceeds in the same manner.

Players alternate turns. If a player draws two addends whose sum has already been colored on the number line, that player loses his turn.

When the facedown stack is depleted, the discard pile is shuffled and play continues until one player colors all the sums.

The first player to color all the sums is the winner.

As children gain experience with this game, have them record the number combinations they encountered at each turn whether or not they were able to color that sum.

Example

0	1	2	3	4	5	6	7	8	9	10
		0 + 2		1 + 3			2 + 5			5 + 5
							6 + 1			

Questions

- What addends are you looking for that would help you color that 6 on the board? Any other addends?

- Were there any sums that were easier or harder to get than others? Which ones? Why do you think that was?

Pyramid

This is a solitaire game. The object is to have the lowest possible score by removing as many cards from the pyramid as possible.

Addition to 10
Kindergarten
Grade 1: CCSS.1.OA.C.6
Grade 2: CCSS.2.OA.B.2

One player

Materials

• ten-frame cards

How to play

The cards are shuffled. Starting at the top of the pyramid, twenty-one cards are arranged faceup in a six-row pyramid with each row overlapping the preceding row. See the sample pyramid below:

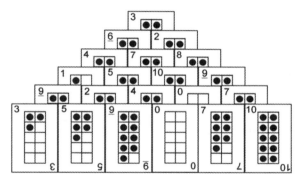

The remaining cards are placed facedown in a stack.

> When children are first learning this game, they will need adult supervision when creating the pyramid, but the children should always be the ones actually building it. As with most tasks, the more often they do it themselves, the better they will be at making it.

Two conditions must be met before a card can be removed:

1. A card must be fully exposed with both bottom corners visible to be playable. When the game begins, only the six cards in the bottom row meet this requirement.

2. Cards can only be removed that equal 10 when their addends are added together.

Example
In the sample pyramid above, only the following cards can be removed:
• *the 7 and the 3 (7 + 3 = 10)*
• *the 10 and the 0 (10 + 0 = 10)*

Example (continued)

After taking the 7, 3, 10, and 0 off the pyramid, there are only four cards that are fully exposed with both bottom corners visible, and none of them combine to equal 10. At this point, no other cards can be removed.

When there are no longer any exposed cards that when added together equal 10, the cards in the facedown stack are used. One card is turned over at a time. It can be used to pair with any fully exposed card in the pyramid to equal 10. If the new card does not combine to equal 10, it is placed in a discard pile, and another card is taken from the facedown stack and the process is repeated.

The game ends when all the cards in the facedown stack have been turned over. A player's score is the number of cards remaining in the pyramid—the fewer cards remaining in the pyramid, the better.

With each game, players try to have fewer cards remaining in the pyramid than in previous games. It is possible to remove all the cards in the pyramid, but it doesn't happen very often.

When children know the combinations of numbers that equal 10, the 10s are taken out of the deck, and a new pyramid is built with the object of finding combinations that equal 9.

Once the children learn the combinations equal to 9, a pyramid to practice the combinations for 8 can be built; however, because the deck is reduced in size, make a smaller pyramid of five rows rather than six.

You can also build the pyramid using six rows to look for combinations that equal 11 or 12.

Some children, when first starting to play this game, may need to count the dots on the ten-frame cards to figure out the sums. That's fine. As they play the game, they'll recognize the addition facts more easily.

At some point, as the children become more experienced with the game, a child might begin to notice that three cards equal 10, such as 6 + 2 + 2. Great! She has noticed an important mathematical concept! **Never tell** the children that this might be a possibility, but allow them to realize it for themselves, and then let them share their discovery with the rest of the players!

Questions

Every time a new card is exposed, ask—

- What do you need to go with that _____?
- Looking at the uncovered cards in the pyramid, what numbers do you hope will be turned over from the stack?

What Does It Take to Get to 10?

The goal of this game is to be the first player to cover three numbers in a vertical, horizontal, or diagonal row.

Addition to 10 (find the missing addend)
Variation: Addition to 12 (find the missing addend)
Kindergarten
Grade 1: CCSS.1.OA.C.6
Grade 2: CCSS.2.OA.B.2

Two players

Materials

- one die

- counters

- "What Does It Take to Get to 10?" game board for each player

4	6	9	7
8	7	5	4
6	4	9	5
7	5	6	8

How to play

Player 1 rolls the die, and figures out what number is needed to get to 10; that is, the difference between the number rolled and 10. He places a counter on one correct game-board number and verbalizes the equation.

Example
Player 1 rolls a 4. A 6 is needed to get to 10. Player 1 covers one of the 6s on the game board and says, "Four plus six equals ten."

Player 2 rolls the die and proceeds in the same manner.

Players alternate turns until one player wins by placing three counters in a vertical, horizontal, or diagonal row.

The purpose of working with missing addends is to introduce children to the basics of algebraic math. If a child knows that 5 + 4 = 9, and she sees a problem stating 5 + __ = 9, she can use this basic knowledge of addends and their sums to begin solving the problem.

For some young children, a 0 to 10 number line might be helpful.

0	1	2	3	4	5	6	7	8	9	10

As children become competent at this game, have them write down the equations they created for each turn on a sheet of paper (see sample below).

Turn 1	4 + 6 = 10
Turn 2	1 + 9 = 10
Turn 3	6 + 4 = 10
Turn 4	5 + 5 = 10
Turn 5	

Questions

- You rolled a _____. How can you figure out how many more are needed to get to 10?

- Can you convince me that _____ is what you need if you rolled a _____?

Variation: Use the "What Does It Take to Get to 12?" game board below to play the game for addition to 12.

8	7	10	7
6	8	9	11
10	9	10	8
7	11	6	9

Addition Concentration

The goal of the game is to find an addends card that equals a sum card.

Addition to 10
Kindergarten
Grade 1: CCSS.1.OA.C.6
Grade 2: CCSS.2.OA.B.2

Two players

Materials

- "Addition Concentration" addends cards
  (cards should be one color)

1 + 0	1 + 1	2 + 1
2 + 2	1 + 4	3 + 3
2 + 5	4 + 4	6 + 3
5 + 5	3 + 0	1 + 3
3 + 2	4 + 2	3 + 4
7 + 1	5 + 4	8 + 2

- "Addition Concentration" sum cards
  (sum cards should be a different color)

1	2	3
4	5	6
7	8	9
10	3	4
5	6	7
8	9	10

Pregame practice

The practice game with the cards *faceup* allows the children to visually see what they are expected to do mathematically.

The addends cards are shuffled and placed faceup in a grid of three rows with six cards in each row.

The sum cards are shuffled and placed faceup to one side of the addends cards in a grid of three rows with six cards in each row.

Player 1 picks an addends card, and then looks for the sum card that equals the addends card. Player 1 verbalizes the equation and takes both cards off the grid.

Example
Player 1 picks up a 6 + 3 addends card and says, "Six plus three equals nine, so I am looking for a nine." She picks up a 9 sums card.

Player 2 proceeds in the same manner.

Players alternate turns, taking matching cards off the grid until all the cards are paired.

How to play

The addends cards are shuffled and placed facedown in a grid of three rows with six cards in each row. The sum cards are shuffled and placed facedown to one side of the addends cards in a grid of three rows with six cards in each.

Player 1 turns over an addends card, leaving it in place, and verbalizes the equation. He turns over a sum card, leaving it in place. If the correct sum card is turned over, Player 1 takes both cards off the board. If the correct sum card is not found, Player 1 turns both cards back over.

Player 2 proceeds in the same manner.

Players alternate turns until all the addends and sum cards have been paired. The players count their accumulated cards; the one with more cards wins the game.

Questions

- What sum card do you need that will equal that addends card?
- Will any other addends card equal that sume card?
- Can you convince me that _____ + _____ equals _____?

Rummy to 10

The object of the game is to be the first player to have three cards that add up to exactly 10.

Addition to 10	**Variation: Addition to 20**
Kindergarten	Grade 1: CCSS.1.OA.C.6
Grade 1: CCSS.1.OA.C.6	Grade 2: CCSS.2.OA.B.2
Grade 2: CCSS.2.OA.B.2	

Two players

Materials

- ten-frame cards 0–4, four of each; the same if using a standard deck

How to play

The cards are shuffled and placed facedown in a stack. The top card is turned faceup and put to the side of the stack to begin a discard pile.

Player 1 takes two cards from the facedown stack and adds the two numbers together to find the sum, and verbalizes the equation to the other player. Player 2 takes two cards and does the same.

Player 1 takes a third card card from either the facedown stack or the discard pile. Player 1 adds the three numbers together and verbalizes the equation to Player 2. If the cards do not equal 10, Player 1 discards one of the cards.

Player 2 proceeds in the same manner.

Players alternate turns until one player's three cards equal 10.

When first playing this game, it may be helpful if everyone plays with her cards faceup on the table. This introduction to the game offers the opportunity for the adult to ask each player a few questions:

- What is the sum of your cards right now?
- Is it greater than ten or less than ten?
- How much more or less will get you to ten?
- What numbers are you looking for that might be helpful?
- What numbers would not be helpful?

Variation: Play "Rummy to 20" with cards 0 to 10. Players take three cards on their first turn. The children are looking for a fourth card that when added to the three cards will result in a sum of 20.

Same Sum

The goal of the game is to find two addends cards with the same sum.

Addition to 7
Kindergarten
Grade 1: CCSS.1.OA.C.6
Grade 2: CCSS.2.OA.B.2

Two players

Materials

- "Same Sum" addends cards

more**4U**

1 + 1	2 + 0	1 + 2	0 + 3
2 + 2	3 + 1	2 + 3	1 + 4
4 + 1	3 + 2	3 + 3	4 + 2
1 + 5	6 + 0	2 + 1	3 + 0
1 + 3	4 + 0	5 + 0	0 + 5
2 + 4	5 + 1	5 + 2	4 + 3

Pregame practice

The practice game with the cards *faceup* allows the children to visually see what they are expected to do mathematically.

The cards are shuffled and arranged faceup in a grid of six rows with four cards in each row.

Player 1 selects a card and verbalizes the equation with its sum to the other player; for instance, "One plus four equals five. I'm looking for another card that equals five." Player 1 finds another card whose sum equals that of the first and again verbalizes the equation to the other player; for example, "Two plus three also equals five." Since both cards have the same sum, Player 1 keeps both cards.

Player 2 selects a card and proceeds in the same manner.

Players alternate turns to find two cards that equal the same sum until all the cards in the grid have been paired.

Children should play the game with the cards faceup until they are familiar with how it is played and begin to know which cards have equal sums.

How to play

The cards are arranged facedown in grid of six rows with four cards in each row.

Player 1 turns over one card, leaving it in place, and verbalizes the equation; for example, "Four plus three equals seven. I'm looking for another card that equals seven." Player 1 turns over a second card, also leaving it in place, and verbalizes that equation. If the sums are equal, Player 1 takes both cards off the grid. If the sums are not equal, both cards are turned back over.

Player 2 turns over a card and proceeds in the same manner.

Play continues until all the cards are paired. The player with more accumulated cards wins the game.

Questions

- Where did you just see a card with that sum?
- If _____ plus _____ equals _____, what other combination of numbers would also equal _____?

Can You Find 11?

This is a solitaire game. The object of the game is to find addends that have a sum of 11.

Addition to 11
Kindergarten
Grade 1: CCSS.1.OA.C.6
Grade 2: CCSS.2.OA.B.2

Variations: Addition from 12 to 20
Grade 1: CCSS.1.OA.C.6
Grade 2: CCSS.2.OA.B.2

One player

Materials

- ten-frame cards,
  0s removed

How to play

The cards are shuffled and placed facedown in a stack.

The player takes the first nine cards and arranges them faceup in a grid of three rows with three cards in each row. The player picks up two or more cards that have a sum of 11 and sets them aside. The player fills the gaps in the grid with cards from the facedown stack. If there are no cards that add up to a sum of 11, the player adds another row of three cards to the bottom of the grid.

The player continues to choose cards that add up to a sum of 11. The game ends when all of the cards in the facedown stack have been used and no remaining cards add up to a sum of 11.

Questions

- What did you notice while playing the game?
- What was the fewest number of cards you needed to make 11? The most?

Variations: The game is played exactly the same way, but players look for cards whose values add up to other sums, such as 12, 13, 14, and so on to 20.

Searching for Sums

The goal of this game is to remove as many counters as possible from the board.

Addition to 12
Kindergarten
Grade 1: CCSS.1.OA.C.6
Grade 2: CCSS.2.OA.B.2

Two players

Materials

- ten-frame cards 1–6, four of each; the same if using a standard deck

- twelve counters for each player

- "Searching for Sums" game board for each player

1	2	3	4	5	6	7	8	9	10	11	12

How to play

The cards are shuffled and placed facedown in a stack. Players place a counter over each number on their game board.

Player 1 takes two cards and adds the numbers for the sum. Player 1 may then remove the counter over the sum, or she may remove the counters over any two numbers that add up to that same sum.

Example
Player 1 draws 5 and 4 from the stack of cards. She may remove the counter above the 9 or the counters above any combination of addends for 9, such as 1 and 8, 2 and 7, 3 and 6, or 5 and 4.

Player 2 draws two cards and proceeds in the same manner.

Players alternate turns. If a player cannot remove any counters that match the sum of the two cards or a combination of addends, the game is over for that player. The other player continues to play until he can no longer remove counters. The player who has removed more counters wins.

Questions

- You just drew _____ and _____. The counter above the sum of those two numbers has already been taken off. Are there any other counters that you could take off?

- Have you discovered a strategy that allows you to take off as many counters as possible?

- Will you try anything different the next time you play this game?

- Were there any sums that were harder to take off than others? Why do you think that might be?

Addition

A Colorful Quilt

The object of the game is to color the most sections on the quilt.

Addition to 12

Kindergarten

Grade 1: CCSS.1.OA.C.6

Grade 2: CCSS.2.OA.B.2

Two players

Materials

- two dice
- crayons or markers in a variety of colors
- "A Colorful Quilt" game board for each player

more4U

1	2	3
4	5	6
7	8	9
10	11	12

Turn 1 2 3 4 5 6 7 8 9 10 11 12

How to play

Player 1 rolls the dice and adds the numbers together. She colors that sum on the game board any color she wishes and crosses off the correct turn number on her game board.

Example
On her first turn, Player 1 rolls a 5 and a 2, and adds them together for the sum of 7. She colors in the 7 square on the quilt and crosses off Turn 1 on her game board.

Player 2 rolls the dice and proceeds in the same manner.

Players alternate turns until each player has had twelve turns. (Players should keep track of turns by crossing off each number as they take that turn.)

If a player rolls a sum whose square has already been colored, that player loses a turn and must cross off that turn number without coloring a square. After twelve turns, the player with the most colorful quilt (the most colored sums) wins.

The above game board is a bit plain. To keep things interesting, children might like to create a quilt with twelve "blocks" that are different shapes, such as triangles or circles.

Questions

- Which sums were easier to color in? Why do you think that is?

- Which sums were harder to color in? Why?

- Was there any sum no one was able to color in? Why do you think that is?

The Three Dice Game

The goal of the game is to be the first player to completely color in any row or column.

Addition to 18 with three addends
Grade 1: CCSS.1.OA.C.6
Grade 2: CCSS.2.OA.B.2

Two players

Materials

- three dice
- one crayon for each player
- "The Three Dice Game" game board for each player

13	5	14	12	2	17	17	12	12	16
16	20	19	9	9	9	9	9	9	9
8	12	10	6	12	14	12	14	12	16
16	8	1	11	3	13	15	2	17	4
11	13	19	10	11	3	13	10	15	13
19	11	5	12	15	14	3	18	6	18
14	12	10	8	8	12	12	10	5	9
7	6	11	12	8	7	11	18	12	11
7	10	4	20	6	12	14	15	1	10
7	20	10	10	13	12	10	4	14	10

How to play

Player 1 rolls the three dice and adds the numbers together. He colors each block in which the sum of the dice appears.

Example
Player 1 rolls a 6, 4, and a 3. He adds 6 + 4 + 3 = 13. He colors all of the 13s on the game board if they have not already been colored.

13	5	14	12	2	17	17	12	12	16
16	20	19	9	9	9	9	9	9	9
8	12	10	6	12	14	12	14	12	16
16	8	1	11	3	13	15	2	17	4
11	13	19	10	11	3	13	10	15	13
19	11	5	12	15	14	3	18	6	18
14	12	10	8	8	12	12	10	5	9
7	6	11	12	8	7	11	18	12	11
7	10	4	20	6	12	14	15	1	10
7	20	10	10	13	12	10	4	14	10

Player 2 rolls the dice and proceeds in the same manner.

The winner is the first player to completely color in any row or column.

Questions

- What sums were easy to get? Why do you think that is?
- What sums were harder to get? Why?

Four-in-a-Row—Sums to 18

The goal of this game is to have four counters in a vertical, horizontal, or diagonal row.

Addition to 18
Grade 1: CCSS.1.OA.C.6
Grade 2: CCSS.2.OA.B.2

Two players

Materials

- two paper clips
- different colored counters for each player
- "Four-in-a-Row" game board

17	2	14	3	8
7	5	0	13	18
1	10	15	6	9
12	8	6	4	7
4	5	3	11	16

0 1 2 3 4 5 6 7 8 9

How to play

Player 1 places two paper clips under any one or two of the addends in the line below the game board. (The two paper clips can be placed under the same addend.)

Player 1 adds the two marked addends and places a counter on one of the corresponding sums on the game board and verbalizes the entire equation to Player 2.

From this point on, only one paper clip can be moved.

Player 2 moves one paper clip to a new addend. She adds these two addends and places a counter on that sum. She verbalizes the entire equation to Player 1.

Example
Player 1 places one paper clip under the 2 and the other under the 6 in the addend line; he adds the numbers together and places a counter on one of the 8s. He says to Player 2, "Two plus six equals eight." Player 2 leaves one paper clip on the 2 and moves the other paper clip to the 9; she adds 2 + 9, and puts a counter on the 11. She says to Player 1, "Two plus nine equals eleven."

If a sum already has a counter on it, another counter may not be put on top.

Players alternate turns until one player has four counters in a vertical, horizontal, or diagonal row.

To introduce this game in the classroom, I play it with the whole class. I use a document camera to project the game board.

I divide the class in half and assign different colors to each side, for instance, the left side of the room (red) plays against the right side of the room (blue). I have found that the round transparent counters available in education supply stores work best.

I'm frequently asked how do I decide which team goes first. There are many possibilities. I always respond, "This is no longer my game. It's yours. You decide. Do what works best for your children."

One team begins the game by telling me where to put the two paper clips. I usually take the first suggestion I hear, but not always. The child must give me a full equation; for example, "Put the first paper clip under the four and the second under the six. Four plus six equals ten." So I put that team's counter on the 10.

The other team has its turn, but they can move only one paper clip. Again, I usually take the first suggestion I hear.

At some point, the students on each team begin to disagree about which paper clip should be moved. I give them a short amount of time, about a minute or so, to get organized, talk about possible strategies, and decide how they are going to proceed.

Once the game is learned as a class, I pair the children to play against each other.

One of the benefits of this game is that it generates a lot of practice in mental addition. Some children may not be ready for that, so it might be helpful to offer them pencil and paper to count, add, or even draw pictures to help them think about what to do next.

Questions

- After looking at the counters already on the board, what sums would be helpful because they would put a counter beside one you already have on the board? What addends could you put your paper clips under that would get you that sum?

- What sum would help you block the other player from getting four counters in a row? Where would you need to put your paper clips to get that sum? Are there other sums that would help you block the other player?

Three Strikes

The goal of this game is to cross off as many sums as possible without striking out.

Addition to 18 with three addends
Grade 1: CCSS.1.OA.C.6
Grade 2: CCSS.2.OA.B.2

Two players

Materials

- three dice
- pencils
- "Three Strikes" game board for each player

3	4	5	6	7	8	9	10	11	12	13	14	15	16	17	18

X X X

How to play

Player 1 rolls the three dice and adds the numbers together. He crosses off that sum on his game board.

Example
Player 1 rolls the dice and 6, 6, and 3 come up. He adds the numbers together and crosses off the 15 on the game board.

Player 2 rolls the three dice and proceeds in the same manner.

If a player rolls a sum already crossed off on her game board, the player receives a strike and circles one of the Xs.

Players alternate turns. The first player to strike out (circles the three Xs) loses the game.

Questions

Stop the players at various points in the game and ask:

- You need a _____. What three numbers might add up to _____?
- Are there any other three numbers that might add up to _____?

Get Close to 20

The object of the game is to create an addition equation with three addends whose sum is as close to 20 as possible. Because this is not an "exact" game, the sum can be more or less than 20.

Addition to 20 with three addends
Variation: Addition to 25 with four addends
Grade 1: CCSS.1.OA.C.6
Grade 2: CCSS.2.OA.B.2

Two players

Materials

- ten-frame cards
- pencils
- "Get Close to 20" recording sheet for each player

Round	Equation	Points for Round
1	+ + =	
2	+ + =	
3	+ + =	
4	+ + =	
5	+ + =	
	Total points for game	

How to play

The cards are shuffled and placed facedown in a stack.

Player 1 takes five cards and uses the numbers on any *three* of the cards to equal a sum that is as close to 20 as possible. Each card can be used only once. Player 1 writes the equation on the recording sheet and puts the five cards in a discard pile.

The points for each round are the *difference* between the sum and 20. For example, a sum of 24 scores four points; a sum of 16 also scores four points.

Player 2 draws five cards and proceeds in the same manner.

When there are no more cards in the facedown stack, the discard pile is shuffled, stacked facedown, and play continues. After five rounds, players find the sum of all their points, and the player with the lesser sum wins.

Questions

- You have five cards, but you can only use three of them. Which three cards will get you as close to 20 as you can get?

- Which two cards don't you need? Why is that?

- Will another combination of three cards you're holding get you any closer? Try out some different combinations.

- Did you find any strategy that helped you get as close to 20 as possible? Which numbers did you find to be helpful? Which numbers were not helpful?

- How did you figure out how close your sums were to 20?

Variation: Change the game to "Get Close to 25." Players take six cards from the stack for each round and use any *four* cards to get a sum as close to 25 as possible.

The Constant Addend

The goal of the game is to have the greater sum.

Addition to 20
Grade 1: CCSS.1.OA.C.6
Grade 2: CCSS.2.OA.B.2

Two players

Materials

- ten-frame cards

How to play

Players are seated side by side, not face to face.

The parent, teacher, or players decide which addition facts need to be practiced, such as +10, +9, +8, and so on, down to +1. Once the fact is determined, a card with that number is taken from the deck and placed between the two players as a constant addend.

The remaining cards are shuffled and divided evenly between the players. The players put their cards facedown in a stack.

Player 1 turns over her top card, adds it to the constant addend, and verbalizes the sum.

Example
Players decide they need to practice +7. They take one 7 out of the deck and place it faceup between each other. This 7 becomes the constant addend in each round. Player 1 turns over a 6, adds it to the 7 in the middle, and says, "Six plus seven equals thirteen."

Player 2 turns over his top card and proceeds in the same manner.

Make sure that the children verbalize their equations. If they don't, they won't actually have to do any addition. They will simply note who drew the greater number, and take both cards based on that.

The player with the greater sum wins both cards. If both players have the same sum (a tie), players turn over one more card and add that number to their previous sum. The player with the greater sum takes all four cards.

The constant addend always stays in the middle and is not picked up by any player.

When all the facedown cards have been used, players count their cards. The player with the most cards wins.

Questions

- What was the most difficult part about this game?
- Do you need more practice with this constant addend?

Stop!

The goal of the game is to be the first player to cover four sums in a vertical, horizontal, or diagonal row.

Addition to 20
Grade 1: CCSS1.OA.C.6
Grade 2: CCSS.2.OA.B.2

Two players

Materials

more**4U**

- counters
- "Stop!" game board for each player

S	T	O	P

- "Stop!" addends cards

0 + 1	1 + 1	3 + 0	1 + 3
2 + 3	4 + 2	2 + 5	7 + 1
5 + 4	2 + 8	8 + 3	6 + 6
8 + 5	5 + 9	9 + 6	8 + 8
7 + 10	9 + 9	9 + 10	10 + 10

How to play

Players write the numbers 1 through 20 anywhere they want on their STOP! game board, one number per box.

The Games

88

The parent or teacher shuffles the addends cards and says, "I will show you an addend card and read it out loud. Cover the sum on your board with a counter."

The adult turns over one card, reads it out loud, and makes sure that every child can see it.

Many children are visual learners and they need to hear and see the numbers.

Urge children to calculate the sum in their heads. Be sure not to verbalize the sum. If one child says the sum out loud, there will be some children who stop and wait for someone to say the sum each time.

The first player to cover four sums in a vertical, horizontal, or diagonal row is the winner.

Questions

- What did you notice while playing the game?

- Will you change anything about the arrangement of your sums on your board for the next game?

Adding Doubles

The goal of this game is to find two cards that are the same—doubles.

Addition to 20: Adding doubles
Grade 1: CCSS1.OA.C.6
Grade 2: CCSS.2.OA.B.2

Two players

Materials

- ten-frame cards 1–10, two of each;
  the same if using a standard deck

- pencils

- "Adding Doubles" recording sheet for each player

Turn	Equation
1	+ =
2	+ =
3	+ =
4	+ =
5	+ =
6	+ =
7	+ =
8	+ =
9	+ =
10	+ =
	Total sum

How to play

The cards are shuffled and arranged facedown in a grid of five rows with four cards in each row.

Player 1 turns over two cards, leaving them in place. If the cards do not match, Player 1 turns them facedown and his turn ends. If the cards match, Player 1 adds the numbers on the cards and writes the addition equation on the recording sheet.

Player 2 turns over two cards and proceeds in the same manner.

Players alternate turns until all the pairs have been found. Each player then adds the sums in the right-hand column of the recording sheet and writes the total sum in the box at the bottom of the sheet. The player with the greater sum wins.

Questions

- How did you figure out the sum of all the doubles you found?

- How can you use doubles to help you learn other addition facts?

Addition

Salute Addition

The goal of the game is to discover the unknown addend.

Addition to 20: finding the missing addend

Grade 1: CCSS.1.OA.C.6

CCSS.1.OA.D.8

Grade 2: CCSS.2.OA.B.2

Two players

Materials

- ten-frame cards

How to play

The cards are shuffled and placed facedown in a stack.

Player 1 turns over the top card and verbalizes the number, then places it faceup so that everyone can see it.

Player 2 draws a card (the "salute" card) and, without looking at it, holds the card on her forehead so that Player 1 can see it, but she can't.

Player 1 mentally adds the two cards and verbalizes the addition equation without revealing the salute number on Player 2's forehead; for example, Player 1 says, "Four plus the number on your head equals ten."

Player 2 must figure out what the card on her forehead is and says that number out loud; in this case, it is six.

Player 2 might be thinking, "I know the first number is four, but I don't know what number is on my head. If the two numbers equal ten, then I must have a six on my head because four plus six equals ten."

If Player 2 answers correctly, she takes both cards. If Player 2 is not correct, she must continue until she figures out the missing addend; however, she will not get to keep the two cards. They are put in a discard pile.

Players reverse roles, and play continues until all the facedown cards have been used. The player with more accumulated cards wins the game.

This is one of my very favorite games!

When we help children learn these very important addition facts to ten, we almost always ask, "What does two plus three equal?" Good to know, but it is also good to teach addition using the missing addend approach: "What number when added to two equals five?"

If you find this is too difficult for your children, start with the cards 1 to 5, four of each.

If a child is having difficulty, try having him put the "salute" card facedown (so it can't be seen) and use counters. "You know you have two counters. How many more will you have to add to the two to get five?" A 0 to 20 number line might also be helpful.

Once children become fairly good at this game, it is important to transfer the equations to a sheet of paper or to the board.

Questions

Explain to the children that n stands for the mystery number on their foreheads, and then ask them a series of questions (sample below), writing everything on a board so they can see it:

- If $5 + n = 9$, what's the mystery number?
- If $n + 5 = 9$, what's the mystery number?

Continue to ask for the mystery number for different equation combinations. Here are a few:

- $9 = 5 + n$
- $9 = n + 5$
- $n + 4 = 9$
- $4 + n = 9$
- $5 + 4 = n$

This game helps children look at and understand what the equals sign means. Too often children only see 4 + 5 = n and think that the equals sign means "now find the answer." They really need to understand that it means that the equation must be balanced or have the same value on each side

Balancing Both Sides

The object of the game is to balance both sides of the equation by arranging the cards into two addition problems with equal sums.

Addition to 20
Grade 1: CCSS.1.OA.C.6
CCSS.1.AO.D.7
Grade 2: CCSS.2.OA.B.2

Two players

Materials

- ten-frame cards
- "Balancing Both Sides" game board for each player

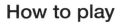
_____ + _____ = _____ + _____

How to play

The cards are shuffled and eight cards are dealt to each player. The remaining cards are stacked facedown. A player earns one point for balancing both sides of the equation.

Player 1 chooses four cards from her hand of eight to place on the game board to create an equal equation. (Players must use at least four cards.) Before taking his turn, Player 2 must check and make sure that Player 1 has balanced both sides of the equation. If so, Player 1 gets one point; she puts her eight cards on the bottom of the stack.

Example
Player 1 has a 9, 7, 4, 5, 4, 3, 1, and 8. She could place 7 + 1 on one side of the equation and 3 + 5 on the other. Player 2 checks the equation. Each side equals eight so both sides of the equation have the same value and the game board is balanced. Player 1 earns one point.

Player 2 chooses four cards from his hand of eight cards to place on his board, and proceeds in the same manner.

Sometimes the eight cards cannot be combined for a balanced equation. That player loses a turn. At other times, there is more than one right combination using the eight cards. In the example above, Player 2 could have also made 5 + 3 = 4 + 4.

The cards are shuffled and each player receives eight new cards. Play continues in the same way.

Players alternate turns, always checking each other's equation to make sure it is balanced.

The game ends when one player reaches ten points.

At some point, it might be helpful if students write their equations on a recording sheet.

Turn	Equations		
1	+	=	+
2	+	=	+
3	+	=	+
4	+	=	+
5	+	=	+
6	+	=	+
7	+	=	+
8	+	=	+
9	+	=	+
10	+	=	+

Some children may eventually realize that a balanced equation need not have the same number of addends, for instance, $3 + 4 = 2 + 2 + 3$. Let the children modify their game boards if they seem ready to handle this discovery.

Questions

- What does the left side of the equation equal? The right side? Are they balanced?
- Is there another way this could be set up using different numbers and still be balanced?

21

In this popular game, players use mental math (no pencil and paper) as they try to reach 21 without going over that sum.

Addition to 21
Grade 1: CCSS1.OA.C.6
Grade 2: CCSS.2.OA.B.2

Two players

Materials

- ten-frame cards

How to play

The game is played for a predetermined period of time. The cards are shuffled. Each player receives one card facedown and one card faceup. (Players take turns being the dealer.)

Keeping the facedown card from the view of the other player, players peek at it and mentally find the sum of their two cards.

Players may ask for one or more additional cards, but must not exceed the sum of 21.

The player whose sum is closest to 21, without going over, is the winner and gets one point. If the players have the same sum, no one gets a point.

At the end of the designated time period, the player with the most points wins the game.

If children have never played this game, it is advisable to play several rounds with all cards faceup so that they can see what they are expected to do.

While there is no set time period for this game, fifteen to twenty minutes of play usually keeps the children engaged, but be alert for any signs of waning interest. If need be, adjust the game session the next time it is played.

Questions

Guide the children through the game with the following questions:

- What is the sum of your numbers now?
- How many do you need to reach 21?
- What number would be best to get?
- What numbers would get you closer to 21 but not there exactly?
- Which numbers would put you over 21?

Reach 25!

The goal of the game is to be the first player to reach 25 *exactly*.

Addition to 25
Grade 1: CCSS1.OA.C.6
Grade 2: CCSS.2.OA.B.2

Two players

Materials

- counters*

- "Reach 25!" game board

5	6	4	3	1	2
3	5	1	2	6	3
2	5	4	1	6	4
5	1	2	3	6	2
1	3	4	5	3	6
4	6	5	4	2	1

* Note: The transparent counters for sale at education supply stores work best for this game. If these counters are not available, have the children place their counters above the numbers.

How to play

Player 1 places one counter on any number on the game board and says the number aloud.

Player 2 places a counter on any number, says the number out loud, then mentally adds it to Player 1's number and verbalizes the sum.

Players alternate turns, mentally adding their number to the previous sum and verbalizing the new sum.

The winner is the first player to reach the sum of 25 exactly.

<u>Variation:</u> The game can be played the same way using different sums as the goal, and the winner be the first player to reach that sum.

Questions

- Did you discover any strategy that was helpful?

- Will you do anything differently the next time you play?

- As you got closer to twenty-five, what were you thinking?

Set It Aside

The goal of the game is to have the greater sum after five rolls of the dice.

Addition to 30 with five addends
Grade 1
Grade 2

Two players

Materials

- five dice
- paper plate for each player
- paper
- pencils

How to play

Each player has only one turn, consisting of five steps:

1. Player 1 rolls the five dice. She puts the die showing the greatest number on her paper plate. If two dice have the same high number, Player 1 puts just one of them on the paper plate. For example, Player 1 rolls a 4, 5, 2, 1, and 5, and she puts one die with a 5 on her paper plate.

2. Player 1 rolls the remaining four dice and again puts the die with the greatest number on her paper plate. There are now two dice on her paper plate.

3. Player 1 rolls the remaining three dice, putting the die with the greatest number on the paper plate.

4. Player 1 then rolls the remaining two dice, putting the die with the greater number on the paper plate.

5. Finally, Player 1 rolls the remaining die and puts it on her paper plate. She writes down the five addends from the dice on her sheet of paper. She adds all five numbers together, and records her final sum for the game.

Player 2 proceeds in the same manner.

The player with the greater sum wins.

Questions

- What is the greatest sum you could possibly get with five dice? Smallest?
- What is the difference between your score and the other player's score? How did you figure it out?

Variations: This game can be modified in a number of ways, but its basic formula remains the same:

- The player with the smaller sum wins.
- Fewer or more dice are used.
- Instead of dice, ten-frame cards 1 to 10, four of each, are used.
- Play continues to a specific number, such as 100.

Estimates or Smart Guesses

This is a silent game—no talking until all five cards are faceup. The goal of the game is to estimate, as closely as possible, the sum of the five addends.

Addition to 25
Grade 1
Grade 2: CCSS.2.OA.B.2

Variation: Addition to 50
Grade 2: CCSS.2.NBT.B.5

Two to six players

Materials

- ten-frame cards, 0–5, four of each, or a standard deck 1–5, four of each

- paper
- pencils

How to play

Players write down their estimates of the sum of the five cards at the top of their papers and circle it, then turn over their papers so as not to reveal their estimate.

After the cards are shuffled and placed facedown in a stack, the players must be silent.

Player 1 turns over the top card and places it faceup for all to see. Player 2 turns over the second card and places it next to the first card. The players mentally add the two numbers to get a sum but do not verbalize the sum, keeping it a "secret."

Example
Player 1 draws a 4. Player 2 draws a 2. All players add 4 + 2 in their heads, keeping the sum (6) to themselves without speaking.

Players continue turning over cards and mentally adding the numbers to the previous sum until five cards are faceup. At this point, players may speak. First, they must agree on the correct sum; then they see whose estimate was closest to the actual sum. That player scores a point for the round.

Example
Player 1 estimates that when all five cards have been drawn, the sum will be 20. Player 2 estimates the sum will be 25. The five cards turned over are 4 + 2 + 5 + 0 + 5 = 16. Player 1's estimate of 20 is closer to the actual sum of 16 than Player 2's estimate of 25. Player 1 scores one point.

At the end of five rounds, the player with the most points wins the game.

I always describe an estimate as a "smart guess." When children begin to play this game, it's unlikely they will have had much experience making estimates, so their estimates won't be very "smart." This game should be played often. It is a great way to give them that experience. After all, as an adult, we make estimates every day of our lives!

Questions

After playing the game a few times, ask these questions:

- What happened at the end of the last game? Was your estimate close to the actual sum?

- Based on what happened in the last few games, how will that affect your estimate for this game?

- Why did you estimate ___? Tell me what you are thinking.

- How did you figure out how close your estimate was to the actual sum?

Variation: The entire deck of ten-frame cards (or cards 1 to 10, four of each, of a standard deck of playing cards) is used to play the game.

Place Value

Introduction

Activity

Paper Clip Stacks 104

Glossary 104

Getting Familiar with the Numbers to 100

Unscramble 105

Tens and Ones 106

Creating and Comparing Two-Digit Numbers

Two-Digit War 108

Who Will Win? 110

Double-Digit Where Does It Belong? 112

Caught in the Middle 114

Close to 50 116

Close to 100 117

Creating and Comparing Three-Digit Numbers

Three-Digit War 109

Three-Digit Who Will Win? 111

Triple-Digit Where Does It Belong? 113

Triple-Digit Caught in the Middle 115

Introduction

Just as names are important to people, place values are important to numbers. Many children, and even some adults, have difficulty comprehending the abstract concept of place value.

To understand place value is to understand the structure and sequence of our base-ten number system. As children count, interpret the values of written and spoken numbers, decide which number is larger or smaller, and explore relationships among numbers, they are developing a mental picture of our number system.

When children count, they learn numbers as a never-ending sequence that goes on and on. With simple counting, children might not catch on to the inherent structure of our base-ten number system. They can count thirteen objects, but they do not see that thirteen is one group of ten and three ones.

A thorough mastery of place value is essential to learning the operations with greater numbers. It is the foundation for regrouping in addition, subtraction, multiplication, and division.

Counting real things, such as marbles and buttons, is one of the best ways to help children build number sense and understand place value. They should begin by counting items by ones, twos, threes, and fives, eventually getting to the all-important tens.

Gradually children begin to realize that if there are lots and lots of objects, the efficient way is to count them in groups, not individually.

Playing the math games in this chapter will enable children to develop a deeper understanding of place value.

Activity

Try this simple activity to introduce counting by tens before playing any games in this section.

Paper Clip Stacks

Make a pile of paper clips (less than a hundred) on the table. Have the children count out ten paper clips and put them in a group. Continue to make groups of ten until no more groups can be made. There will probably be some paper clips left over—these are the ones. Ask the children how many groups of ten were counted and how many ones were left.

Example
A pile of paper clips is counted out into six stacks of ten and four units of one each. Ask the children, "How many groups of ten did you count? How many ones were left? What does six tens and four ones equal? Can you count the piles of paper clips by tens and ones (10, 20, 30, 40, 50, 60, 61, 62, 63, 64)?"

Count lots of different objects this way.

Place Value Glossary

When playing any math games, it is important that the children become familiar with the correct math terminology for certain facts and concepts. In this section there is one word that is used in many of the games. It should be consistently used; its definition is below.

Digit is a symbol used to indicate a numeric value. For example:

- 8 is a one-digit number
- 18 is a two-digit number
- 180 is a three-digit number

Unscramble!

The goal of this game is to put the numbers 1 to 100 in order from least to greatest. This is not a timed, "beat the clock," game. The assumption is that children will become faster at sorting the cards the more often they play, and they'll begin to see more patterns that will help them tackle more complex math concepts.

Getting familiar with numbers 1–100

Kindergarten

Grade 1

Grade 2

One or two players

Materials

- one set of "Unscramble!" 1–100 cards for each player

How to play

The players should have a generous area to sort their cards, such as a table or other flat surface. Players shuffle their cards and put them in a pile.

On the "Go" signal, players put their cards in order from 1 to 100.

This is an incredible activity to watch—all those strategies (or lack thereof)! I make no comments, even though I may see some students going about their task very inefficiently. Children usually begin by ordering the numbers using very unproductive methods. For instance, it is not uncommon for a child to spend a great deal of time hunting for the 1, and then searching for the 2, and so on. After playing this game several times, they usually come to the realization that there just might be a faster, more efficient way to accomplish the task.

Every once in awhile, I will ask the children to stop and walk around the room and carefully look at how other players are arranging their numbers.

Several days later, we play the game again, and I note who is going about the task in a more efficient fashion. It might be helpful for some children to have a large hundred chart visible.

Questions

- Can you explain how you are going about this task?

- Did it take you a shorter or longer amount of time to sort the cards today than the other day?

- What comes after 42? Before 95?

Tens and Ones

The goal of the game is to be the first player to land on 100 *exactly*.

Getting familiar with a hundred board
Kindergarten
Grade 1: CCSS.1.NBT.C.5
Grade 2

Two players

Materials

- counter for each player
- die
- hundred board for each player

1	2	3	4	5	6	7	8	9	10
11	12	13	14	15	16	17	18	19	20
21	22	23	24	25	26	27	28	29	30
31	32	33	34	35	36	37	38	39	40
41	42	43	44	45	46	47	48	49	50
51	52	53	54	55	56	57	58	59	60
61	62	63	64	65	66	67	68	69	70
71	72	73	74	75	76	77	78	79	80
81	82	83	84	85	86	87	88	89	90
91	92	93	94	95	96	97	98	99	100

- "Tens and Ones" Rules for Rolling sign

Rules for Rolling

Roll a 1 or a 2, move FORWARD 10 spaces.

Roll a 3 or a 4, move FORWARD 1 space.

Roll a 5, move BACK 1 space.

Roll a 6, move BACK 10 spaces.

How to play

Players put a counter just before the 1 on their hundred boards.

Player 1 rolls the die and moves his counter on his board according to the Rules for Rolling, and tells Player 2 the number he landed on. Player 2 rolls the die and proceeds in the same manner.

Players alternate turns. If a player cannot move her counter as indicated by the roll of the die, she loses her turn. The winner is the first player to reach 100 exactly.

Example
Player 2 lands on 91 and rolls a 2 on her next turn, she loses a turn because 91 + 10 places her game piece at 101 and off the board. Players may not move their counters past 100.

When children begin to play this game, they may have to count each space if they roll a 1 or 2 to move ten spaces forward or a 6 to move ten spaces back. Eventually, they may begin to notice patterns in the hundred board. They won't have to count the spaces, but they'll simply move from 54 to 64, for example.

Questions

• What have you noticed about the hundred board while playing this game?

• Have you noticed any patterns on the hundred board?

Variations: After playing "Tens and Ones" several times, make eleven copies of the hundred board for each child. Using one board for each task below, ask the children to color—

    1. all the even numbers;

    2. all the odd numbers;

    3. all the single-digit numbers;

    4. all the double-digit numbers;

    5. all the numbers with a 0 in them;

    6. all the numbers that have a 4 in them;

    7. all the numbers that have a 7 in the ones place;

    8. all the numbers that have a 2 in the tens place;

    9. all the numbers where the digits are the same;

   10. all the numbers where both digits added together equal 10; and

   11. all the numbers where the first digit is greater than the second.

Questions: After each task is completed and the hundred board colored in, ask:

    • Why do you think it looks like this?

    • What patterns do you see?

Two-Digit War

The goal of each round of this game is to be the player with the greater two-digit number.

Creating and comparing two-digit numbers

Variation 1: Creating and comparing two-digit numbers
Grade 1: CCSS.1.NBT.B.3
Grade 2

Variation 2: Creating and comparing three-digit numbers
Grade 2: CCSS.2.NBT.A.4

Two players

Materials

- ten-frame cards with 10s removed
  or a standard deck with 10s and face cards removed

- "Two-Digit War" game board for each player

Tens	Ones

How to play

The cards are shuffled and placed facedown in a stack.

Player 1 turns over one card and decides whether to put it in the tens or ones column on his board. The card must be placed before the other player can take a turn. Once down, it *cannot* be moved.

Player 2 turns over one card and decides whether to put it in the tens or ones column on her board.

Player 1 turns over a second card and puts it in the empty column. Player 2 turns over a second card and does the same.

Players read their numbers out loud to each other; for example, Player 1 says, "I have eight tens and seven ones. I have eighty-seven". Player 2 says, "I have seven tens and two ones. I have seventy-two."

The player with the greater two-digit number takes all four cards.

If the players have built the same two-digit number (a tie), players build a second two-digit number to break the tie. The player with the higher number takes all eight cards.

Play continues until all the cards in the stack have been used. Players count their accumulated cards, and the player with more cards wins.

As the children become more adept at using tens and ones, they should begin to record the results of each round (see the sample recording sheet below). This will give the children an opportunity to use the greater than, less than, and equal to symbols.

Round	Player 1	>=<	Player 2
Sample	87	>	72
Sample	45	<	47
Sample	53	=	53

Questions

- Have you found a strategy that helps you create a greater two-digit number?

- In order to win this round, what number will your second card need to be?

- Are there any numbers that will not be helpful?

- You say you're hoping for a _____. How likely is it that you will draw a _____?

Variation 1: The game is played in the same way, but the player with the smaller (lesser) number wins.

Variation 2: Modify the game to play "Three-Digit War." Each player takes three cards and tries to make the greater three-digit number using the game board below. Players read their numbers out loud to each other, using the number of the card in each column to express hundreds, tens, and ones, and the resulting three-digit number.

Hundreds	Tens	Ones

Who Will Win?

The goal of this game is to make the greater or smaller two-digit number.

Creating and comparing two-digit numbers
Grade 1: CCSS.1.NBT.B.3
Grade 2

Variation: Creating and comparing three-digit numbers
Grade 1
Grade 2 CCSS.2.NBT.A.4

Two players

Materials

- ten-frame cards with 10s removed,
  or a standard deck with 10s and face cards removed

- one coin

How to play

The cards are shuffled and placed facedown in a stack.

Player 1 takes two cards and turns them over for Player 2 to see. He verbalizes both possible numbers he can make and his choice as to which two-digit number he will make.

Example
Player 1 turns over a 9 and a 4. He says, "I can make either 94 or 49. I'm going to make 94."

Player 2 takes two cards and does the same.

Player 1 flips the coin to determine who will win a point. If the coin comes up—
- heads, the lesser number wins a point;
- tails, the greater number wins a point.

Players alternate turns. At the end of each round, the four used cards are put in a discard pile. The first player to accumulate ten points is the winner.

Questions

- What is the difference between _____ and _____?

- Can you prove to me that _____ is greater than _____?

- How many tens in _____? How many ones?

- How many ones in _____? How many tens?

- Could you draw a _____ that would show what [any number, e.g., 43] means?

Variation: "Three-Digit Who Will Win?" is played the same way, but the players take three cards and build a three-digit number.

Double-Digit Where Does It Belong?

The goal of the game is to be the first player to fill in each space on the recording sheet with an appropriate two-digit number.

Creating and comparing two-digit numbers
Grade 1: CCSS.1.NBT.B.3
Grade 2

Variation: Creating and comparing three-digit numbers
Grade 2: CCSS.2.NBT.A.4

Two players

Materials

- ten-frame cards with 10s removed,
  or a standard deck with 10s and face cards removed

- "Double-Digit Where Does It Belong?" recording sheet
  (If using a standard deck, cross out the 00–09 line on the recording sheet.)

Step Number	Actual Number
00–09	
10–19	
20–29	
30–39	
40–49	
50–59	
60–69	
70–79	
80–89	
90–99	

How to play

The cards are shuffled and placed facedown in a stack.

Player 1 turns over two cards and tells Player 2 what two double-digit numbers are possible to create, and then states what number she has decided to make. Once Player 1 has made her choice, she writes that number in the appropriate space on her recording sheet.

Example
Player 1 turns over a 3 and a 6. She tells Player 2, "I can make either 36 or 63. I have decided to make 36." She records it on the line for 30–39 because 36 falls between 30 and 39.

Player 2 draws two cards and proceeds in the same manner.

Players continue to alternate turns. If a player cannot put either possible number on a line because that line is already filled, he loses a turn.

The first player to get all the spaces filled is the winner.

Questions

- Why did you decide to make _____ instead of _____?

- Which sections on the recording sheet still need a number? What numbers would fit on the _____ – _____ line? Which would not?

Variation: "Triple-Digit Where Does It Belong?" is played in the same way, but each player draws three cards, decides on a three-digit number to make, and places it on the correct line (see the recording sheet below).

Step Number	Actual Number
000–099	
100–199	
200–299	
300–399	
400–499	
500–599	
600–699	
700–799	
800–899	
900–999	

Caught in the Middle

The goal of this game is to have the third two-digit number fall between a player's smallest two-digit number and greatest two-digit number.

Creating and comparing two-digit numbers
Grade 1: CCSS.1.NBT.B.3
Grade 2

Variation: Creating and comparing three-digit numbers
Grade 2: CCSS.2.NBT.A.4

Two players

Materials

- ten-frame cards with 10s removed
  or a standard deck with 10s and face cards removed

How to play

The cards are shuffled and placed facedown in a stack.

Player 1 takes four cards to make two two-digit numbers. She uses two of the cards to make the smallest possible two-digit number, and then uses the remaining two cards to make the greatest two-digit number.

Player 2 takes four cards and proceeds in the same manner.

Example
Player 1 draws a 6, 2, 7, and 1. She uses the 1 and 2 to make the smallest two-digit number she can, a 12. She uses the 6 and 7 to make the greatest possible two-digit number, 76. The range of Player 1's two numbers is 12 to 76. Player 2 draws a 5, 3, 1, and 4. He uses the 1 and 3 to make the smallest two-digit number he can, 13, and uses the other two cards to make the greatest two-digit number possible, 54. The range of Player 2's two numbers is 13 to 54.

After both players make their two-digit numbers, two more cards are turned over. The first card turned over is the *tens* number. The second card is the *ones* number.

Players only score a point if this new number falls between the two they have made.

Example
Using the example above, Player 1's range of numbers is 12 to 76, and Player 2's is 13 to 54. The last two cards turned over are a 6 for tens and a 2 for ones. The point number is therefore 62. Player 1 scores a point because 62 is between 12 and 76. Player 2 does not score a point because 62 does not fall between 13 and 54.

The ten cards are placed in a discard pile. When there are no more cards in the facedown stack, the discard pile is shuffled and the game continues.

Players continue to alternate turns. The first player to reach twenty points is the winner.

Questions

- What numbers come between your two numbers?
- What numbers come before your smallest number?
- What numbers come after your greatest number?

Variation: "Triple-Digit Caught in the Middle" is played in the same manner, but players take six cards to create two three-digit numbers with as wide a range as possible. After both players make their three-digit numbers, three more cards are turned over. The first card turned over is the *hundreds* number; the second card is the *tens* number; and the third card is the *ones* number.

Place Value

Close to 50

The goal of this game is to create a two-digit number that is as close to 50 as possible.

Creating and comparing two-digit numbers
Grade 1: CCSS.1.NBT.B.3
Grade 2

Variation: Creating and comparing three-digit numbers
Grade 2: CCSS.2.NBT.A.4

Two players

Materials

- ten-frame cards with 10s removed
  or a standard deck with 10s and face cards removed

How to play

The cards are shuffled and placed facedown in a pile.

Player 1 takes two cards from the pile and, basing her decision on which of the two numbers will be closest to 50, she chooses which card will be the *tens* and which card will be the *ones*.

Example
Player 1 draws a 4 and an 8. She knows she can make 48 or 84, and decides to make 48 because that is closer to 50 than 84.

Player 2 takes two cards from the pile and proceeds in the same manner.

The player whose number is closest to 50 takes all four cards. If there is a tie and both players are an equal distance from 50, they each keep their own two cards.

When all the facedown cards are used, the player with more accumulated cards wins.

It might be very helpful if children had a hundred chart plus paper and pencils to figure out how close their numbers are to 50.

If the number is less than 50, an adult's instinct about how the task should be done might be to subtract that number from 50 to find the difference, for example, 50 - 32 = 18, or if the number is greater than 50, to subtract 50 from that number, 84 – 50 = 34, for instance. But many children (and adults) might find it easier to count up from 32 to 50 or from 50 to 84. That's all right, too.

Questions

- How can you figure out what the difference is between ___ and 50?

- Why did you choose _____ over _____?

- Convince me that _____ is closer to 50 than _____.

- What numbers might be closer to 50 than your number?

Variation: "Close to 100" is played in the same manner, but players draw two cards to create a number as close to 100 as possible.

The Games

Multidigit Addition

Introduction

Glossary 120

Two-Digit Plus One-Digit Addition

    The Teens Game 121

    Race to 100 123

    Addition Action 124

Two-Digit Addition with No Regrouping

    Double-Digit Addition 126

Two-Digit Addition with Regrouping

    Concentration 100 128

    Get As Close As You Can to 50 130

    Get As Close As You Can to 100 131

    Beat the Teacher 132

    It All Adds Up 134

Three-Digit Addition with Regrouping

    Triple-Digit Addition 127

    Three-Digit Beat the Teacher 133

    Triple-Digit It All Adds Up 135

Introduction

The basic concepts of addition are typically taught in kindergarten, but it's usually at the end of first grade that children start adding two-digit numbers in the classroom. They build upon this skill in second grade with the introduction of regrouping (borrowing and carrying).

It is enormously important and helpful for children to understand place value concepts before they tackle multidigit addition or subtraction. If they do not, even children who calculate correctly may show little understanding of the procedures they are using.

There is a strategy for doing multidigit addition. It is called partial-sums, or front-end, addition. I like it because it puts the emphasis on understanding place value. This front-end strategy is particularly helpful if you are doing mental math. Here is an example:

$$
\begin{array}{r}
136 \\
+198 \\
\hline
334
\end{array}
\qquad
\begin{array}{rcrcrr}
100 & + & 100 & = & 200 & 200 \\
30 & + & 90 & = & 120 & 120 \\
6 & + & 8 & = & 14 & +14 \\
& & & & & \hline
& & & & & 334
\end{array}
$$

Regrouping, or the column-addition method, is another strategy used by many teachers, adults, and children. Often the understanding of place value is overlooked when teaching this method. This can be partially addressed by discussing the addition of the ones, then the tens, then hundreds, and so on, as follows:

Example
As you write a three-digit addition problem on the board or a piece of paper, talk through the process:

When adding numbers in columns such as

$$236$$
$$\underline{+153}$$

Keep in mind that—

* *you are first adding six ones (6) and three ones (3);*
* *when you get to the tens, you are not adding 3 and 5, you are actually adding three tens (30) and five tens (50); and*
* *in the same way, you are not adding 2 plus 1 in the hundreds column, but are adding two hundreds (200) plus one hundred (100).*

Build in understanding by noting place values when playing these multidigit addition games.

Some of the games toward the end of this section may be more appropriate for a third grader, but they have been included for those children who are ready for the challenge.

Multidigit Addition Glossary

When playing any math games, it is important that the children become familiar with the correct math terminology for certain facts and concepts. In this section there are five words that should be consistently used; their definitions are below.

Digit is a symbol (numeral) used to indicate a numeric value. For example, 8 is a one-digit number, 18 is a two-digit number, and 180 is a three-digit number.

Addend is any number added to another to get a sum or total.

Sum is the total (whole amount) realized as a result of adding numbers (addends).

Equal is having the same amount or identical value.

Equation, sometimes called a number sentence, is a mathematical statement containing an equals sign, which shows that two expressions are equal.

addend		addend	equals sign	sum		
31	+	16	=	47		

addend		addend	equals sign	addend		addend
40	+	30	=	50	+	20

The Teens Game

The goal of the game is to be the first player to put all 20 counters on the board.

Two-digit plus one-digit addition: 10 to 19
Kindergarten: CCSS.K.NBT.C.4
Grade 1: CCSS.1.OA.C.6
CCSS.1.NBT.B.2b
Grade 2: CCSS.2.OA.B.2

Two to four players

Materials

- 20 counters for each player

- "The Teens Game" number cards 11–19

11	12	13
14	15	16
17	18	19
11	12	13
14	15	16
17	18	19

more4U

- "The Teens Game" game boards 1, 2, 3, and 4; a different one for each player

Game Board 1

10	5	10	2
9	10	1	10
10	6	10	3
4	10	7	10
10	2	10	9
8	10	5	10

Game Board 2

5	10	3	10
10	8	10	2
4	10	7	10
10	9	10	5
3	10	1	10
10	6	10	8

Game Board 3

10	8	10	1
4	10	3	10
10	5	10	9
2	10	8	10
10	7	10	4
1	10	6	10

Game Board 4

3	10	7	10
10	4	10	6
8	10	1	10
10	5	10	3
7	10	2	10
10	9	10	6

How to play

The number cards are shuffled and placed facedown in a stack.

Player 1 takes a card and says the number out loud. Looking at his board, Player 1 places one counter on each of two numbers that when added together will equal the number on his card (the sum). He then says the equation out loud. The card is placed in a discard pile.

Example
Player 1 draws 16. Looking at his game board, he places a counter on the 10 and one on the 6. He then verbalizes the equation, "Ten plus six equals sixteen."

Player 2 takes the next card and proceeds in the same manner.

If the number (sum) on the card cannot be made, that player loses a turn.

The winner is the player who first puts all twenty counters on the board.

When all the cards in the facedown stack have been used, the discard pile is shuffled and used again.

Questions

• What did you discover as a result of playing this game?

• What is the meaning of the number _____?

Race to 100

The goal of this game is to be the first player to either reach or pass 100.

Two-digit plus one-digit addition to 100
Grade 1: CCSS.1.NBT.C.4
Grade 2: CCSS.2.NBT.B.5

Two players

Materials

- one die
- paper
- pencils

How to play

Player 1 rolls the die and records the number at the top of her paper. Player 2 rolls the die and does the same.

Players continue to alternate rolls, adding the subsequent numbers to their previous sum. After each turn, players must check each other's addition for accuracy.

The first player to reach 100 or more is the winner.

Questions

- What was easy about this game?
- What was more difficult?

Variation 1: The game is similar, but players must hit 100 exactly. For example, if a player has 98, she needs a 2 to win the game. If she does not roll the needed number, she must wait for her next turn.

Variation 2: The game is played in the same way, but ten-frame cards are used instead of the die.

Variation 3: This version of the game inserts another addition task into the game. Two dice are rolled, and the results are added together to create the number to be added to the previous sum.

Addition Action

The goal of this game is to make the greater sum.

Two-digit plus one-digit addition
Grade 1: CCSS.1.NBT.C.4
Grade 2: CCSS.2.NBT.B.5

Two players

Materials

- ten-frame cards 0–4, four of each,
  or a standard deck 1–4, four of each

- paper
- pencils

How to play

The cards are shuffled and placed facedown in a stack. Players take turns drawing a card until both players have three cards.

Players arrange their cards to make a two-digit plus one-digit addition problem with the greatest possible sum.

When players are satisfied with their arrangements, they write down their problem and find the sum. Players exchange papers to check each other's addition for accuracy. The player with the greater sum scores a point.

Example
Player 1 draws 3, 3, and 4. He sets up his problem as:

$$\begin{array}{r} 43 \\ +3 \\ \hline 46 \end{array}$$

Player 2 draws 2, 1, and 4. She sets up her problem as:

$$\begin{array}{r} 42 \\ +1 \\ \hline 43 \end{array}$$

The players check each other's work for addition accuracy. Player 2 earns one point because her sum of 46 is greater than the sum of 43.

The used cards are put in a discard pile. Players take three new cards, and play continues. The first player to accumulate ten points is the winner of the game.

Questions

- Can you make a greater sum by arranging your numbers in a different way? Try it.

- Prove to me that you made the greatest sum possible using those three numbers.

- One of you had the greater sum. Why? What made the difference?

Variation 1: The game is played in the same way but the player with the smaller sum wins.

Variation 2: The game can be modified to incorporate regrouping by using ten-frame cards 0 to 9.

Double-Digit Addition

The goal of this game is to create the greatest sum possible using four cards.

Two-digit addition with no regrouping

Variation 1: Two-digit addition with no regrouping

Variation 2: Two-digit addition with regrouping
Grade 1
Grade 2 CCSS.2.NBT.B.5

Variation 3: Three-digit addition
Grade 2 CCSS.2.NBT.B.7

The Games

Two players

Materials

- ten-frame cards 0–4, four of each,
  or a standard deck 1–4, four of each

- paper

- pencils

How to play

The cards are shuffled and placed facedown in a stack. Players alternate taking a card until both have four cards.

Players arrange their four cards into a two-digit addition problem that will give them the greatest sum possible. When the players finish arranging their cards, they write down the problem and find the sum. Players exchange papers and check each other's addition.

Example
Player 1 draws 4, 1, 3, and 0 and writes down

$$\begin{array}{r} 41 \\ + \underline{30} \\ 71 \end{array}$$

Player 2 draws 2, 0, 3, and 2 and writes down

$$\begin{array}{r} 32 \\ + \underline{20} \\ 52 \end{array}$$

The player with the greater sum scores a point.

The used cards are put in a discard pile. Each player takes four new cards and play continues. When then are no more facedown cards, the discard pile is shuffled, placed facedown, and the game proceeds.

The first player to earn ten points is the winner.

Questions

- Why did you decide to arrange your numbers as you did? What were you thinking?

- Can you arrange your numbers in a different way so your sum will be even greater?

- If you had to make the least sum, would you change your strategy? How?

Variation 1: The game is played the same way, but the player with the lesser sum wins.

Variation 2: The game is played in the same manner, but cards 0 to 9 are used.

Variation 3: "Triple-Digit Addition" is played in a similar manner using cards 0 to 9. Each player draws six cards and creates two three-digit numbers that when added together will create the greatest sum possible.

Concentration 100

The goal of this game is to find two numbers that when added together equal 100.

Two-digit addition with regrouping
Grade 1
Grade 2: CCSS.2.NBT.B.5

Two players

Materials

- "Concentration 100" addend cards

10	90	25	75	33	67
47	53	55	45	2	98
76	24	88	12	5	95
40	60	15	85	77	23
30	70	92	8	61	39

Pregame practice

The practice session with the cards *faceup* allows the children to see what they are expected to do mathematically.

The cards are shuffled and placed faceup in a grid of five rows with six cards in each row.

Player 1 finds two addend cards whose sum is 100 and sets them aside.

Player 2 finds two addend cards whose sum is 100 and sets them aside.

Players alternate turns until all the matches have been made.

Questions

- What do you need to go with that _____?

- What could you do to figure it out?

- Are there any combinations that you knew immediately equaled 100?

How to play

The cards are shuffled and placed facedown in a grid of five rows with six cards in each row.

Player 1 turns over one card, leaving it in place, and says the number out loud. She turns over a second card and says that number out loud. If the cards equal 100, Player 1 verbalizes the equation; for example, "Twenty-five plus seventy-five equals one hundred," and keeps both cards. If the cards don't equal 100, Player 1 tells Player 2 what they do equal; for instance, "Twenty-five plus thirty-three does not equal one hundred, they equal fifty-eight." She turns the cards back over, leaving them in the same place.

Player 2 takes a turn and proceeds in the same manner.

When players find a match and keep both cards, they do not immediately get another turn as in some games. Players continue to alternate turns so that all players stay engaged.

Players alternate turns until all the matches have been made. The winner is the player with more accumulated cards.

When they first start to play this game, children may need to use paper and pencil to figure out which card they need. Over time, the paper and pencil may not be needed as often, if at all.

Questions

• After children have turned over the first addend, ask them which card they are looking for that when added to the first card will make a sum of 100.

• What can you do to figure out which card you need?

Get As Close As You Can to 50

The object of the game is to make a two-digit addition problem whose sum comes as close to 50 as possible. Sums are allowed to be more than 50.

Two-digit addition with regrouping
Grade 1
Grade 2: CCSS.2.NBT.B.5

Two players

Materials

- ten-frame cards, 0–5, four of each, or a standard deck 1–5, four of each

- paper

- pencils

How to play

The cards are shuffled and placed facedown in a stack.

Player 1 takes four cards. She arranges the cards to create a two-digit addition problem whose sum will be as close to 50 as possible, and then writes down the problem and sum on paper. Player 2 checks for addition accuracy.

Example
Player 1 draws 1, 3, 2, and 4 from the stack. She tries out various arrangements until she decides that the closest she can get is—

$$
\begin{array}{cc}
41 & 43 \\
+\,13 \quad \text{or} \quad & +\,11 \\
\hline
54 & 54
\end{array}
$$

Player 2 draws four cards and his turn proceeds in the same manner.

The points for each round are the *difference* between a player's sum and 50. In the example above, Player 1 scores 4 points, but a sum of 46 would also score 4 points.

After the players have recorded their points, they put their four cards in a discard pile.

For the second round, Player 2 begins first. Players alternate starting positions after each round.

After six rounds, players total their points and the player with the lowest score wins.

Questions

- Have you discovered a strategy that will help you get your sum as close to 50 as possible?

- Why did you arrange your cards the way you did? Tell me what you were thinking.

- If you moved the cards around, could you make a problem whose sum is closer to 50?

- How did you figure out how close to 50 your sum is?

Variation: Modify the game to play "Get As Close As You Can to 100." Use cards 0 to 9 (1 to 9 if using a standard deck). The object of the game is to make a two-digit addition problem whose sum comes as close to 100 as possible. The sum can be over 100.

Beat the Teacher

This is a group game that can be played by the whole class. The object of this game is to get a sum greater than the teacher's or parent's sum.

Two-digit addition with regrouping

Variation 1: Two-digit addition with regrouping
Grade 1
Grade 2: CCSS.2.NBT.B.5

Variation 2: Three-digit addition
Grade 2: CCSS.2.NBT.B.7

Materials

- two-digit addition grid for each player
- die
- paper
- pencils

The first time you play this game, don't tell the children what the goal is. Let them put their numbers anywhere they choose. Once they've finished the first round, tell them that the only way to win is to have a sum greater than yours. Then ask them if they will change their strategy in the next round. Play a second round, and then ask them what they did differently.

How to play

The teacher draws a large grid on the board (see below) for all to see. The children draw the same grid on their papers. (Grids may also be downloaded and printed, if desired.) The teacher also has a paper grid for his personal use. The game is played for a predetermined amount of time.

The teacher rolls the die four times. Each time the die is rolled, the teacher calls out the number, and the children must immediately put the number into any one of the top four spaces on the grid. **Once written, the number cannot be moved to a different space.** Do not put any numbers in the bottom two spaces.

The teacher does the same on his paper grid but does not reveal his placement of the numbers to the class.

> I often check to make sure the children are immediately writing the number in a space. Also, if necessary, make them play the game with a pen or crayons so they are not tempted to move the number to a different space later in the game.

When all four top spaces have been filled, everyone completes the two-digit addition problem and places the sum in the bottom two spaces. Players check each other's addition for accuracy.

The teacher reveals his paper grid and fills the spaces of the grid on the board with his numbers and his sum. Students who have a sum that is greater than the teacher's sum "beat the teacher" and get two points. Students who have a sum equal to the teacher's sum get one point; students with a sum less than the teacher's do not earn any points.

At the end of the game session, the players with the most points are the winners.

Questions

- What strategies have you discovered that will help you make a greater sum?
- Why do you think your strategy worked?
- Will you use the same strategies if you have to make a sum less than the teacher's?

<u>Variation 1:</u> The game is played the same way, but the players with a sum less than the teacher's win two points.

<u>Variation 2:</u> "Three-Digit Beat the Teacher" is played in a similar manner but the die is rolled six times, and players make two three-digit numbers for the greatest sum. (Sample grid is below.)

+

It All Adds Up

Here's a way to play "Beat the Teacher" without the teacher! Creating an addition problem with the greatest sum possible is still the object of the game.

Two-digit addition with regrouping

Variations 1 and 2: Two-digit addition with regrouping
Grade 1
Grade 2: CCSS.2.NBT.B.5

Variation 3: Three-digit addition
Grade 2: CCSS.2.NBT.B.7

Two players

Materials

- ten-frame cards with 10s removed
  or a standard deck with 10s and face cards removed

- two-digit addition grid for each player

- paper

- pencils

How to play

The game is played to a predetermined number of points to win. The players draw a grid like the one below. (Grids may also be downloaded and printed, if desired.)

```
        |
 _____|_____
        |
 +      |
 _____|_____
        |
        |
```

The cards are shuffled and placed facedown in a stack.

Player 1 draws a card that is placed faceup for both players to see. Players write this number in one of the top four spaces on their grid. The number must be written down immediately on the grid. **Once written, it cannot be moved to a different space.** Do not put numbers in the bottom two spaces.

Player 2 draws a card that is placed faceup for both players to see. The players select one of the remaining top three spaces on their grid and write the number in it.

Players alternate drawing a card until four cards have been turned over. When all four top spaces have been filled, players complete the two-digit addition problem, writing the sum in the bottom two spaces.

Players trade papers and check each other's addition. The player with the greater sum is the winner of that round and scores one point. The first player to reach the agreed upon score wins.

Questions

- Have you discovered a strategy for placing your numbers that will give you the greatest sum?

- Why do you think your strategy worked?

- Is that the same strategy you would use if you were trying to make the smallest sum? Why or why not?

- What did the other player do differently that gave her the greater sum?

Variation 1: The game is played in the same way, but the player with the lesser sum wins the round.

Variation 2: The player whose sum is closest to 50 wins the round; otherwise, the game is played in the same way.

Variation 3: "Triple-Digit It All Adds Up" is played using three-digit addition, and players draw six cards each. (Sample grid is below.)

+

The Games

Subtraction

Introduction

Glossary.. 138

One-Digit Subtraction to 6

    Very Simple Subtraction 139

    Find One Less 140

One-Digit Subtraction to 10

    One Less 142

    Subtract! 143

    Target Subtraction... 145

    More: A Game of Differences.. 146

    Subtraction Ladder.. 147

    Four-in-a-Row Subtraction 149

One-Digit Subtraction from 100

    Begin with 100 151

    Going Down (or Up)! 153

Two-Digit Subtraction

    Going Down (or Up) from 500 154

    Double Subtraction.. 155

    1,000 to None... 157

Introduction

Building math skills can be compared to a table with four legs. In building math skills, addition, subtraction, multiplication, and division are the legs. As with any table, when one leg is faulty or breaks, that table is of little use. Without a thorough understanding of subtraction, children won't have a sturdy foundation on which to develop more complex math abilities.

Subtraction is taking a number or a quantity away from another number or quantity, and this concept can be perplexing for young children. Part of the challenge for children lies in the fact that subtraction is often taught by starting with abstract ideas—12 minus 9 equals 3. Young children need to begin with a more concrete approach: Count out 12 cubes, take away 9, and count how many are left.

Children's difficulties with subtraction illustrate the necessity of making connections between subtraction and addition. If a child knows that 3 + 4 = 7, then he will more readily perceive that 7 − 3 = 4. When the recall of addition facts is automatic and students understand the connection between addition and subtraction facts, their fluency with subtraction facts naturally increases.

If children cannot make the connection between addition and subtraction, then they have to resort to learning by rote. As children are given more opportunities to realize how addition and subtraction are related, they will become more secure in their understanding of both. And using real, physical objects to instruct these difficult concepts will support children's learning by connecting the ideas to what they can see and know.

Example
Rather than just writing 3 + 4 = 7 and 7 − 4 = 3 on a board, put three paper clips in a plate, and then add four more. Ask the class to tell you how many paper clips are in the plate, and write the equation 3 + 4 = 7 for the children to see. Then take away four paper clips, and ask the class to tell you how many are left in the plate. Write 7 − 4 = 3 on the board as well.

To attain fluency with subtraction facts, children need ongoing opportunities to practice them—something the following games will provide—and with that, the games will also help develop students' understanding of subtraction.

Subtraction Glossary

When playing any math games, it is important that the children become familiar with the correct math terminology for certain facts and concepts. In this section there are four words that should be introduced and consistently used; their definitions are below.

Digit is a symbol used to indicate a numeric value. For example:

5 is a one-digit number.

15 is a two-digit number.

150 is a three-digit number.

Difference is the amount by which two numbers differ in quantity or the answer to a subtraction problem.

difference
↓
10 − 5 = 5

Equal is having the same amount or identical value.

Equation, sometimes called a number sentence, is a mathematical statement that contains an equals sign, indicating that the two expressions are equal.

10 − 5 = 5

5 = 10 − 5

9 − 4 = 10 − 5

Very Simple Subtraction

The goal of the game is to remove all the counters above all the numbers (differences) on the number line.

One-digit subtraction
Kindergarten: CCSS.K.OA.A.5
Grade 1: CCSS.1.OA.C.6
Grade 2: CCSS.2.OA.B.2

Two players

Materials

- two dice
- six counters for each player
- "Very Simple Subtraction" 0–5 number line for each player

0	1	2	3	4	5

How to play

Players put a counter under each number (difference) on their number line.

Player 1 rolls the dice and subtracts the smaller number from the greater number, and removes the counter below the correct difference on her number line.

Example
Player 1 rolls a 3 and a 5. She subtracts 3 from 5 (5 – 3) to get the difference (2), and removes the counter below the 2 on her number line.

Player 2 rolls the dice and proceeds in the same manner.

Players alternate turns. When players get a difference that is already uncovered, they lose that turn.

The first player to uncover all the differences on their number line is the winner.

It might be helpful for young children to use counters such as pennies or buttons to make this experience more concrete. For example, if they roll a 5 and a 3, they take five counters and then subtract (take away) three of them to discover how many are left.

Questions

- What did you discover while playing this game?
- Were there any differences that were easier to uncover than others?

Find One Less

The goal of the game is to put ten counters on numbers that are one less than the roll of the die.

One-digit subtraction
Kindergarten: CCSS.K.OA.A.5
Grade 1: CCSS.1.OA.C.6
Grade 2: CCSS.2.OA.B.2

Two players

Materials

- one die
- pencils
- ten counters for each player
- "Find One Less" game grid for each player

How to play

Before playing the game, each player randomly writes five 0s, five 1s, five 2s, five 3s, five 4s, and five 5s in their grid, one number per square (see sample below).

0	1	2	3	4	5
2	3	3	4	0	1
3	0	5	1	5	4
1	5	4	5	2	0
4	2	0	3	1	2

Player 1 rolls the die and puts one counter one of on the numbers that is one less than the roll of the die. Player 2 rolls the die and proceeds in the same manner.

Example
Player 1 rolls a 5 and puts a counter on one of the 4s. Player 2 rolls a 3 and puts a counter on one of the 2s.

If a player rolls the die and he cannot put a counter on the number that is one less than the rolled number, the player loses a turn.

The first player to put all ten counters on the board wins the game.

When I first discovered this game, I hesitated to use it because I thought that subtracting 1 from any number would be much too easy for my first graders. I could not have been more wrong! Many of the children struggled with this concept. I quickly learned that this is typical for young children.

I decided to give everyone counters. When they rolled the die, they took that many counters. Then they subtracted 1 counter and counted what was left. It helped! Soon they didn't need the counters.

Using a 0 to 10 number line might be helpful, too.

0	1	2	3	4	5	6	7	8	9	10

Question

- What helped you while playing this game?

One Less

The goal of this game is to find two cards where the number on one card is one less than the number on the other card.

One-digit subtraction
Kindergarten
Grade 1: CCSS.1.OA.C.6
Grade 2: CCSS.2.OA.B.2

Two players

Materials

- ten-frame cards with 0s removed, or a standard deck 1–10, four of each

How to play

Players sit side by side. The cards are shuffled and placed facedown in a stack.

Player 1 takes ten cards and places them faceup in a line between both players.

Player 1 looks for two cards with a difference of one. When he finds two such cards, he says, "I can take these cards because _____ is one less than _____."

Player 2 adds two more cards to the faceup line. (The line always has ten cards.) She hunts for two cards with a difference of one.

If there are no cards in the line with a difference of one, another card is added to the line.

Players alternate turns until all the facedown cards have been added to the line and all possible "one-less" combinations have been made.

Counters or a 0 to 10 number line might be very helpful so that children can visualize what they are being asked to do.

0	1	2	3	4	5	6	7	8	9	10

Question

- Can you prove to me that one less than _____ is _____?

Variations: "Two Less" and "Three Less" are played in a similar manner.

Subtract!

The goal of this game is to have the smaller difference.

One-digit subtraction
Kindergarten
Grade 1: CCSS.1.OA.C.6
Grade 2: CCSS.2.OA.B.2

Two players

Materials

- ten-frame cards
- "Subtract!" recording sheet

How to play

The cards are shuffled and placed facedown in a stack.

Player 1 turns over two cards and subtracts the smaller number from the greater number. Player 2 turns over two cards and does the same.

The player with the smaller difference wins all four cards.

Example
Player 1 draws 4 and 7. She subtracts the 4 from the 7 to get a difference of 3. Player 2 draws 9 and 8. He subtracts the 8 from the 9 to get a difference of 1. Player 2 wins the round and takes all four cards because 1 is a smaller difference than 3.

In the event that both players have the same difference (a tie), each player takes two more cards and subtracts the smaller number from the greater number. The player with the smaller difference wins all eight cards.

Players alternate turns until all the facedown cards have been used. The players count their cards. The player with the greater number of cards is the winner.

After children begin to understand the game, it is important that they record what happened in each round (see the sample recording sheet below).

	Player 1		Player 2
Turn	Equation	> = <	Equation
1	8 – 3 = 5	>	9 – 7 = 2
2	5 – 4 = 1	<	3 – 0 = 3
3	10 – 4 = 6	>	9 – 7 = 2
4	8 – 2 = 6	=	10 – 4 = 6

Questions

- How did you figure out the difference between your two numbers?

- If your goal is to make the smallest difference possible, what kind of numbers are you looking for?

- If your goal is making the greatest difference possible, what kind of numbers are you looking for?

Target Subtraction

The goal of this game is to find two numbers that when subtracted from each other equal the target difference.

One-digit subtraction
Kindergarten
Grade 1: CCSS.1.OA.C.6
Grade 2: CCSS.2.OA.B.2

Two players

Materials

- ten-frame cards
- target difference board

Target Difference

How to play

The cards are shuffled and placed facedown in a stack.

Player 1 takes one card and places it faceup on the target difference board between the players.

The remaining cards are arranged faceup so that all are visible.

Player 2 looks for two cards that when the smaller number is subtracted from the greater number the difference will equal the target difference. After Player 2 selects his cards, he puts them to the side, and Player 1 proceeds in the same manner.

Example
Player 1 draws a 6 and lays it faceup on the target difference board. Player 2 looks for two cards that will make a subtraction fact that has a difference equal to 6, such as 10 – 4, 9 – 3, 8 – 2, 7 – 1, or 6 – 0.

Players alternate turns looking for two cards whose difference equals the target. When no more combinations can be found, the cards are shuffled and Player 2 draws a card for a different target difference so that play can continue.

Questions

- How do you know that you have found all the combinations that equal _____?
- What are all the combinations that equal _____?

More: A Game of Differences

The goal of this game is to practice finding differences using randomly selected numbers.

One-digit subtraction	**Variation: Two-digit subtraction**
Kindergarten	Grade 2: CCSS.2.NBT.B.5
Grade 1: CCSS.1.OA.C.6	
Grade 2: CCSS.2.OA.B.2	

Two players

Materials

- ten-frame cards
- counters

more**4**U

How to play

The cards are shuffled and put facedown in a stack.

Each player turns over one card. Players decide who has the greater number, and then figure out how much "more" that player has. The player who has "more" takes the quantity of counters that equals the difference between the two players' numbers.

Example
Player 1 turns over a 3. Player 2 turns over a 9. Player 2 has the greater number, which is 6 more than Player 1's, so Player 2 takes 6 counters.

Play continues until all the cards have been drawn. Players count their counters, and the player with more counters wins the game.

Questions

- What have you noticed while playing this game?
- Convince me that _____ is that much more than _____.
- When you take a lot of counters in a turn, what do you notice about the two numbers drawn?
- What do you notice about the amount of counters you get when both numbers are close together?

Variation: Each player turns over two cards and makes the greatest two-digit number possible. The players then determine who has the greater number, and using pencil and paper, figure out the difference between the two numbers. The player who has "more" gives himself points equal to the difference between the two numbers. When all the cards in the facedown stack are gone, the player with more points wins the game.

Example
Player 1 draws a 6 and a 7, and makes 76. Player 2 draws a 1 and a 3, and makes 31. Player 1 has the greater number, in this case, 45 more, so Player 1 scores 45 points for this round.

Subtraction Ladder

The goal of this game is to create subtraction equations that allow a player to put an equation on all the rungs of the ladder.

One-digit subtraction
Kindergarten
Grade 1: CCSS.1.OA.C.6
Grade 2: CCSS.2.OA.B.2

Two players

Materials

- ten-frame cards
- "Subtraction Ladder" recording sheet
- paper
- pencils

How to play

Each player draws a ladder with nine rungs on his sheet of paper. (Recording sheet may be downloaded and printed, if desired.)

= 9
= 8
= 7
= 6
= 5
= 4
= 3
= 2
= 1

The cards are shuffled and placed facedown in a stack. Player 1 takes five cards and puts them faceup in a line.

Player 1 selects two of these cards to make the left side of an equation that has a difference between 1 and 9, and writes it on the appropriate rung of her ladder.

Subtraction

Example
Player 1 draws 5, 9, 1, 3, and 3. She decides to make 9 – 5 and writes it on the 4 rung of her ladder.

	= 9
	= 8
	= 7
	= 6
	= 5
9 – 5	= 4
	= 3
	= 2
	= 1

Player 1 puts the two used cards in a discard pile.

Player 2 draws five cards and puts them faceup in a line and proceeds in the same manner.

Players can put only one equation on each line. If a player cannot make an equation, that player picks two cards from his line to put in the discard pile, and loses that turn.

Before taking their next turn, the players draw two more cards from the facedown stack so that they always have five cards to work with.

It may seem awkward not to have the children take their two cards at an earlier point in the game, but I have found that if children immediately draw two more cards, they focus on those two cards and not on the current action of the other player.

Players alternate turns until one player wins by filling in all nine rungs on her ladder.

If the cards in the facedown stack run out, the discard pile is shuffled, stacked facedown, and play continues.

Questions

- What did you discover while playing this game?
- Were there any differences that were more difficult to make? Why?
- What equations could you use that would equal _____?
- What's a strategy you might try in the next game?

Four-in-a-Row Subtraction

This game generates a lot of mental subtraction practice. Its goal is to have four counters in a vertical, horizontal, or diagonal row.

One-digit subtraction
Kindergarten
Grade 1: CCSS.1.OA.C.6
Grade 2: CCSS.2.OA.B.2

Two players

Materials

- two paper clips
- different counters for each player
- "Four-in-a-Row Subtraction" game board

7	2	4	3	6
3	5	0	7	8
1	0	5	6	9
2	8	6	4	7
4	5	3	1	8

0 1 2 3 4 5 6 7 8 9

How to play

Player 1 places two paper clips under any two of the numbers in the line below the game grid. The two paper clips can be placed under the same number.

Player 1 subtracts the smaller number from the greater number and places one of her counters on one of the corresponding differences on the game grid.

Example
Player 1 places one paper clip under the 4 and the other under the 2. She subtracts 4 – 2, and places a counter on one of the 2s in the grid.

From this point on, only one paper clip can be moved.

Player 2 moves one paper clip under a new number. He subtracts the smaller number from the greater number, and places a counter on that difference.

Example
Continuing the example above, Player 2 leaves one paper clip on the 2 and moves the other paper clip to the 9. He subtracts 9 – 2, and puts one of his counters on one of the 7s in the grid.

If a difference already has a counter on it, another counter may not be put on top.

Players alternate turns in this manner until one player has four counters in a vertical, horizontal, or diagonal row.

Questions

- After looking at the counters already on the board, what differences would be helpful because they would get another counter beside one you already have on the board?

- What numbers might you use to get that difference? Are there any other numbers that you might use?

- What differences would help you block the other player from getting four in a row?

When I introduce this game at school, I play it with the whole class. I use a document camera to project the game board, including the number line.

I divide the class in half and the left side of the room (red) plays against the right side of the room (blue). I have found that round transparent counters, available at many education supply stores, work best. (I'm often asked how do I decide which team goes first. There are many possibilities. I always respond, "This is no longer my game. It's yours. You decide. Do what works best for your children.")

One team begins the game by telling me where to put the two paper clips. Almost always, I take the first suggestion I hear. The suggestion maker must give me a full equation, for instance, "Put the first paper clip under the 4 and the second under the 6. 6 minus 4 equals 2." So I put that team's counter on the 2 in the grid to which they direct me.

It's now the other team's turn, but they can move only one paper clip. Again, I take the first suggestion I hear.

At some point, the students on both teams begin to disagree about which paper clip should be moved. I give them a short time, a minute or two, to get organized, talk about possible strategies, and decide how they are going to proceed.

Once the game is learned, I put them in pairs, and they play against each other with paper copies of the game board, counters, and two paper clips.

Begin with 100

The goal of this game is to be the first player to reach or pass 0.

One-digit subtraction from 100
Grade 2: CCSS.2.NBT.B.5

Two players

Materials

- ten-frame cards
- paper
- pencils

How to play

The cards are shuffled and placed facedown in a stack.

Player 1 writes 100 at the top of his paper. He then draws one card and subtracts this number from 100. He places the card in a discard pile. Player 2 checks Player 1's subtraction and initials it if correct.

Example
Player 1 draws a 4 and writes on his paper:

$$\begin{array}{r} 100 \\ -4 \\ \hline 96 \end{array}$$

Player 2 checks his subtraction and initials it.

Player 2 writes 100 at the top of her paper and then proceeds in the same manner. When all the cards in the facedown stack have been used, the discard pile is shuffled and play continues. Players alternate turns until one player reaches or passes 0.

Because this game allows play to go beyond zero, it often offers children a casual and non-threatening encounter with negative numbers. I don't go into negative numbers at this time unless children ask, and then I just explain that like "regular" numbers (positive numbers), negative numbers go on forever. As play approaches zero, it is helpful to have a –10 to +10 number line so children can visualize subtraction that results in a negative number.

-10	-9	-8	-7	-6	-5	-4	-3	-2	-1	0	1	2	3	4	5	6	7	8	9	10

Questions

- What do you notice about playing this game?

- If you want to be the first player to reach zero, what are the best numbers to draw?

- What was the most difficult part of playing this game? The easiest?

Going Down (or Up)!

The goal of this game is to be the first player to reach or pass 0.

One-digit subtraction from 100
Grade 2: CCSS.2.NBT.B.5

Variation: Two-digit subtraction from 500
Grade 2

Two players

Materials

- die
- paper
- pencils

How to play

Players write 100 at the top of their papers.

Player 1 rolls the die and subtracts that number from 100. Player 2 checks Player 1's subtraction and initials it if correct.

Example
Player 1 rolls a 5 and and writes on his paper:

        100
      -   5
         95

Player 2 checks his subtraction and initials it.

Player 2 takes her turn, and play proceeds in the same manner, with players alternating turns and checking each other's subtraction.

There's only one complication! When a 6 is rolled, the rules change. Players don't subtract. Instead, they add 6 to their total.

Example
Player 2 rolls a 6 and she writes on her paper:

        100
      +   6
        106

Player 1 checks her addition and initials it.

The first player to reach or pass 0 wins the game.

Because this game allows play to go beyond zero, it often offers children a casual and non-threatening encounter with negative numbers. I don't go into negative numbers at this time unless children ask, and then I just explain that like "regular" numbers (positive numbers), negative numbers go on forever. As play approaches zero, it is helpful to have a –10 to +10 number line so children can visualize subtraction that results in a negative number.

-10	-9	-8	-7	-6	-5	-4	-3	-2	-1	0	1	2	3	4	5	6	7	8	9	10

Questions

- What have you noticed about playing this game?

- If you want to reach 0 first, what are the best numbers to roll?

Variation: Two dice are used in "Going Down (or Up) from 500." The game proceeds in a similar manner to "Going Down (or Up)!" but players make a two-digit number to subtract from 500. **There's one complication: When one of the dies comes up as a 1, the rules change. Players don't subtract. Instead they add the two-digit number to their total.** The first person to reach or pass 0 wins.

Don't tell the children which two-digit number they should use. Let them discover and share why it is in their best interest to make the greatest two-digit number when subtracting and the smallest two-digit number when adding. Trust them—someone will notice!

Questions:
- If you are subtracting, how did you decide which two-digit number to use?

- Will you use that same strategy if you have to add? Why or why not?

- What was the most challenging part of this game?

Double Subtraction

The object of this game is to make two-digit subtraction problems with the smallest possible differences.

Two-digit subtraction

Variation 1: Two-digit subtraction
Grade 2: CCSS.2.NBT.B.5

Variation 2: Three-digit subtraction
Grade 2

Two players

Materials

- ten-frame cards with 10s removed,
  or a standard deck with 10s and face cards removed

more**4U**

- paper
- pencils

How to play

The cards are shuffled and put facedown in a stack.

Player 1 takes four cards and arranges them to make a two-digit subtraction problem that will have the smallest possible difference. Player 2 checks Player 1's subtraction and initials it if correct. Player 1 places her four cards in a discard pile.

Example
Player 1 draws 7, 5, 1, and 8. She moves the cards around, and decides to make 81 and 75. She writes down on her paper:

$$\begin{array}{r} 81 \\ -\ 75 \\ \hline 6 \end{array}$$

Player 2 checks her subtraction and initials it.

Player 2 takes four cards and play proceeds in the same manner. The players then compare their results. The player with the smaller difference scores one point.

Players alternate turns. When all the cards in the facedown stack have been used, the discard pile is shuffled and play continues. The first player to score ten points is the winner.

Questions

- Why did you decide to arrange your numbers the way you did?
- Could you arrange your numbers in another way and make a smaller difference?

Questions (continued)

- Have you discovered a strategy that helps you arrange your numbers to make the smallest difference?

- Would this strategy work if you were trying to make the greatest difference? Try it and find out.

Variation 1: The game is played in a similar manner, but the players create two-digit subtraction problems that have the greatest differences possible.

Variation 2: The game is modified so that each player draws six cards to make three-digit subtraction problems that have the smallest or greatest differences possible. You decide the goal.

The Games

1,000 to None

The goal of this game is to be the first player to reach or pass 0.

Two-digit subtraction
Grade 2: CCCS.2.NBT.B.5

Two players

Materials

- ten-frame cards with 10s removed,
  or a standard deck with 10s and face cards removed
- paper
- pencils

How to play

The cards are shuffled and stacked facedown. Players write 1,000 at the top of their papers.

Player 1 draws two cards and decides which two-digit number to make. He subtracts it from 1,000. Player 2 checks Player 1's subtraction and initials it if correct. Player 1 puts the two cards in a discard pile.

Example
Player 1 turns over a 9 and a 3. He can make either 39 or 93 and subtract it from 1,000. He writes on his paper:

   1,000

− 93

    907

Player 2 checks his subtraction and initials it.

Do not tell the children which two-digit number to use. Let them discover and share why it is in their best interest to make the greatest two-digit number when subtracting. Trust them—someone will notice!

Player 2 turns over two cards and play proceeds in the same manner.

Players alternate turns. When all the cards in the facedown stack have been used, the discard pile is shuffled and play continues.

The first player to reach or pass 0 wins.

Because this game allows play to go beyond zero, it often offers children a casual and non-threatening encounter with negative numbers. I don't go into negative numbers at this time unless children ask, and then I just explain that like "regular" numbers (positive numbers), negative numbers go on forever. As play approaches zero, it is helpful to have a –10 to +10 number line so children can visualize subtraction that results in a negative number.

-10	-9	-8	-7	-6	-5	-4	-3	-2	-1	0	1	2	3	4	5	6	7	8	9	10

Questions

- Did you find a strategy that helped you when subtracting?
- Since you are subtracting, how did you decide which two-digit number to use?

Multiple Operations in One Game

Introduction

One-Digit Addition and One-Digit Subtraction

Target—0 160

Sums and Differences 162

Add or Subtract? 163

Add, Subtract, or Do Both! 165

Addition and Subtraction Snap 167

Are They Equal? 168

Balancing Both Sides—Addition and Subtraction 170

Exactly 25 172

The Double Ladder Game 173

The Ten-Card Game 175

Two-Digit Addition and Subtraction

Benchmark Numbers 177

Introduction

In real-life activities, we frequently do various combinations of adding and subtracting. When we buy a car, follow a recipe, or decorate our home, we use adding and subtracting almost simultaneously. But when we do mathematics in school, oftentimes we do just one operation and then move on to another. When doing so, there's no indication that all of these operations are interrelated or that they will be used together as we live our lives.

So let's get real and play some games where players are required to use both adding and subtracting in various ways.

Target—0

The object of the game is to be the first player to reach 0 *exactly*. Very young children can play this game without recording the equations.

One-digit addition

One-digit subtraction
Kindergarten: CCSS.K.OA.A.3
Grade 1: CCSS.1.OA.C.6
Grade 2: CCSS.2.OA.B.2

Two players

Materials

- different game piece for each player
- one die
- "Target—0" game board for each player

| 20 |
| 19 |
| 18 |
| 17 |
| 16 |
| 15 |
| 14 |
| 13 |
| 12 |
| 11 |
| 10 |
| 9 |
| 8 |
| 7 |
| 6 |
| 5 |
| 4 |
| 3 |
| 2 |
| 1 |

-10	-9	-8	-7	-6	-5	-4	-3	-2	-1	0

- "Target—0" recording sheet for each player

Turn	Equation
1	20 – =
2	
3	
4	
5	
6	
7	
8	
9	
10	

How to play

Each player puts her game piece on the game board at 20.

Player 1 rolls the die and moves her game piece the number of spaces indicated on the die. She writes the equation on her recording sheet; for example, 20 – 4 = 16.

Player 2 rolls the die and proceeds in the same manner.

Players alternate turns. The winner of the game is the first player to land exactly on 0. Players will likely move back and forth between positive and negative numbers until one player lands exactly on 0.

This game introduces negative numbers in a casual and nonthreatening way. Children in kindergarten through second grade can play this game easily. I don't usually go into negative numbers at this time, unless they ask, and then I usually just explain that like positive numbers ("regular" numbers), negative numbers go on forever.

Questions

- What do you need to roll that will get you to 0 exactly?
- Will any other number get you almost there?
- What numbers would take you beyond 0?
- After the players roll the die, but before they move, ask them to tell you where they will end up.

Sums and Differences

The goal of this game is to have the greater grand total of sums and the lesser grand total of differences at the end of ten turns.

One-digit addition

One-digit subtraction

Kindergarten: CCSS.K.OA.A.3

Grade 1: CCSS.1.OA.C.6

Grade 2: CCSS.2.OA.B.2

Two players

Materials

- two dice
- "Sums and Differences" recording sheet for each player

Turn	Die 1	Die 2	Sum	Difference
1				
2				
3				
4				
5				
6				
7				
8				
9				
10				
			Grand Total	Grand Total

How to play

Player 1 rolls the first die and records the number; then he rolls the second die and records that number. Player 1 writes the equations for the sum and difference of these two numbers and reads both equations to Player 2, who checks both for accuracy.

Example

Player 1 rolls 2 and 6; he records:

Turn	Die 1	Die 2	Sum	Difference
1	2	6	$2 + 6 = 8$	$6 - 2 = 4$

Player 2 rolls both dice and proceeds in the same manner.

At the end of ten turns, both players add their ten sums. The player with the greater grand total of sums is the "sum" winner. Both players then add their ten differences. The player with the lesser grand total of differences is the "differences" winner.

The Games

Add or Subtract?

The goal of this game is to have three counters in a vertical, horizontal, or diagonal row.

One-digit addition

One-digit subtraction

Kindergarten: CCSS.K.OA.A.3

Grade 1: CCSS.1.OA.C.6

Grade 2: CCSS.2.OA.B.2

Two players

Materials

- different counters for each player

- ten-frame cards 1–5, four of each;
  the same if using a standard deck

- pencils

- "Add or Subtract?" game board

7	5	3	10
2	9	6	1
6	4	2	7
1	3	8	0
4	1	5	2

- "Add or Subtract?" recording sheet for each player

Turn	Addition Equation	Subtraction Equation
1		
2		
3		
4		
5		
6		
7		
8		
9		
10		

How to play

The cards are shuffled and placed facedown in a stack.

Player 1 draws two cards and writes both the addition and subtraction equations on the recording sheet. He chooses the addition or subtraction equation and circles it, and then places a counter on the resulting sum or difference on the game board. Player 1 must verbalize the equation to Player 2 to show her why he is putting the counter on that number.

Example
Player 1 draws 2 and 5. He could cover a 3 by using the equation 5 – 2 = 3 or a 7 using 2 + 5 = 7. He writes both equations on his recording sheet. Player 1 decides to use 5 – 2 = 3, so he circles that equation on his recording sheet, and puts a counter on one of the 3s. He tells Player 2, "Five minus two equals three."

Player 2 draws two cards and proceeds in the same manner.

Players alternate turns until one player has three counters in a vertical, horizontal, or diagonal row.

Questions

- What did you notice while playing this game?
- What prompted you to choose to add or subtract?

The Games

Add, Subtract, or Do Both!

The game's object is to create an addition or subtraction fact that equals the game number.

One-digit addition

One-digit subtraction
Kindergarten: CCSS.K.OA.A.3
Grade 1: CCSS.1.OA.C.6
Grade 2: CCSS.2.OA.B.2

One to six players

Materials

- ten-frame cards

- pencils

- game number board

Game Number

- Add, Subtract, or Do Both! recording sheet for each player

The Game Number is _____	
Turn	Equation
1	
2	
3	
4	
5	
6	
7	

How to play

The cards are shuffled and placed facedown in a pile. Player 1 draws one card and puts it on the game-number board. The board is put between the players. The remaining cards are spread faceup around the game number.

Player 1 finds two (or more) cards whose numbers equal the game number either through addition or subtraction, and records the equation on her recording sheet. Player 2 checks the equation for accuracy. Player 1 puts the cards in a discard pile.

Example
The game number is 7. Players have several choices they might use:

2 and 5 to make 2 + 5 = 7

1, 2, and 4 to make 1 + 2 + 4 = 7

10 and 3 to make 10 − 3 = 7

8, 2, and 1 to make 8 − 2 + 1 = 7, and so on

Player 2 proceeds in the same manner.

Players take turns finding numbers that when added or subtracted equal the game number. When all possible combinations have been removed from the board, the game is over.

Players go over their recording sheets and figure out their scores. Players get—
- one point for every plus sign (+) they used; and
- two points for every minus sign (−) they used.

The player with more points wins the game.

Questions

- What did you discover while playing this game?

- Which did you tend to do more often, add or subtract? Why?

- Could you add and subtract in the same equation?

Variation: Players must use at least three cards to create an addition or subtraction equation that equals the game number.

Addition and Subtraction Snap

The goal of the game is to be the first player to say the correct difference out loud.

One-digit addition

One-digit subtraction

Kindergarten: CCSS.K.OA.A.3

Grade 1: CCSS.1.OA.C.6

Grade 2: CCSS.2.OA.B.2

Two players

Materials

- ten-frame cards

How to play

The cards are shuffled and placed facedown in a stack.

Player 1 turns over one card. Both players silently double the number in their heads. Player 1 turns over a second card. The players mentally subtract the smaller number from the larger number. The first player to say the correct difference out loud gets one point.

Example

Player 1 turns over the first card; it is a 6. Both players double the number (6 + 6 = 12) mentally. Player 1 turns over a second card; it is a 5. The smaller number is subtracted from the greater number, in this case, 12 – 5 = 7. The players who says, "Seven," first wins a point.

If there is a tie, both players get a point. If there is a disagreement on the correct difference, players work together to figure out the correct answer. The player who was correct gets one point. The two used cards are put in a discard pile.

Player 2 picks a card and play proceeds in the same manner.

Play continues until all the cards in the facedown stack has been used. The player with the most points is the winner.

Questions

- What did you discover about yourself while playing this game?
- What are your strengths? What do you do well? What do you know well?
- What do you need to practice?

Are They Equal?

The goal of this game is to find an addition fact card and a subtraction fact card whose sum and difference are equal (have the same value).

One-digit addition

One-digit subtraction

Kindergarten: CCSS.K.OA.A.3

Grade 1: CCSS.1.OA.C.6

Grade 2: CCSS.2.OA.B.2

Two players

Materials

- "Are They Equal?" addition fact cards

4 + 3	5 + 1	2 + 3
3 + 1	1 + 2	2 + 0
1 + 1	2 + 5	4 + 2
0 + 5	2 + 2	2 + 1
3 + 3	1 + 3	0 + 3

- "Are They Equal?" subtraction fact cards

10 – 3	11 – 5	7 – 3
9 – 4	8 – 4	7 – 1
9 – 6	12 – 10	8 – 5
9 – 7	11 – 4	5 – 2
8 – 2	10 – 5	10 – 6

Pregame practice

The practice session with the cards *faceup* allows the children to see what they are expected to do mathematically.

The addition cards are shuffled and then turned faceup in a grid of three rows with five cards in each row. To one side of the addition cards, the subtraction cards are handled in the same manner.

Players take turns finding one addition fact card whose sum equals the difference of one subtraction fact card. When a player has selected an addition card, she verbalizes the equation, including the sum, and then states what corresponding subtraction card she needs. Once she finds it, she takes both cards and verbalizes the equation for the other player.

Example
Player 1 picks up the addition card 4 + 3 and says, "Four plus three equals seven. I am looking for a subtraction card whose difference equals seven." She finds 10 − 3 and says to the other player, "Ten minus three equals seven. Because both equations equal seven, I can say four plus three equals ten minus three."

Player 2 selects an addition card and play proceeds in the same manner with players alternating turns until all the addition and subtraction cards are matched.

How to play

Turn all the addition fact cards facedown in a grid of three rows with five cards in each row. To one side of the addition cards, the subtraction fact cards are handled in the same manner.

Player 1 turns over one addition card, keeping it in place, and reads it aloud with its sum to the other player, then states what corresponding subtraction card he needs. Player 1 turns over one subtraction card, keeping it in place.

If Player 1 finds a subtraction fact whose difference has the same value as the sum of his addition fact, he keeps both cards and verbalizes the complete equation for Player 2. If the sum and difference do not have the same value, both cards are turned back over, and it is Player 2's turn.

Player 2 turns over an addition card and play proceeds in the same manner with players alternating turns until all the cards are matched. The player with more cards wins the game.

Question

- If you're looking for subtraction fact card whose difference has the same value as that sum, what number combinations might you find?

Variation: The game is played in a similar way, but it is modified so that players turn over the subtraction fact first, and then must find an addition fact card whose sum is equal to the difference of the subtraction fact.

Question: If you're looking for an addition fact card whose sum has the same value as that difference, what sum combinations might you find?

Balancing Both Sides— Addition and Subtraction

The object of the game is to balance both sides of the equation by arranging the cards to create one addition problem and one subtraction problem with a sum and difference of equal value.

One-digit addition

One-digit subtraction

Kindergarten: CCSS.K.OA.A.3

Grade 1: CCSS.1.OA.C.6

Grade 2: CCSS.2.OA.B.2

Two players

Materials

- ten-frame cards
- "Balancing Both Sides—Addition and Subtraction" game board for each player

_____ + _____ = _____ − _____

How to play

The cards are shuffled and dealt. (Players take turns being the dealer.) Each player gets eight cards. The remaining cards are stacked facedown between the two players.

Player 1 chooses four cards from her hand to place on the game board to make a balanced equation. **Players must use four cards.** A player earns one point for balancing the equation.

Example
Player 1's eight cards are 9, 7, 4, 5, 4, 3, 1, and 8. She could place 5 + 3 on one side of the equals sign and 9 − 1 on the other (5 + 3 = 9 − 1). Both facts equal 8 (5 + 3 = 8 and 9 − 1 = 8), so both sides of the equation have the same value, and the game board is balanced.

Player 2 must check the addition and subtraction facts to make sure that Player 1 has balanced her game board. If she has, Player 1 gets one point. Her eight cards are placed at the bottom of the facedown stack.

Player 2 chooses four cards from his hand of eight to place on the board, and play continues in the same manner, with his cards also placed at the bottom of the facedown stack.

After each round of play, the cards are shuffled and each player gets eight new cards for the next round. Play continues in the same manner, with players always checking each other's board to make sure that the equation is balanced.

Sometimes the eight cards cannot be arranged in a balanced equation, so the player loses a turn, placing his cards at the bottom of the facedown stack.

The game ends when one player reaches ten points.

Questions

- What does the left side of the equation equal? Right side? Are they balanced? Do they have the same value?

- Is there another way this could have been set up using different numbers and still be balanced?

Exactly 25

The goal of the game is to be the first player to reach 25 *exactly*.

One-digit addition

One-digit subtraction
Kindergarten: CCSS.K.OA.A.3
Grade 1: CCSS.1.OA.C.6
Grade 2: CCSS.2.OA.B.2

Two players

Materials

- ten-frame cards
- paper
- pencils

more4-U

How to play

The cards are shuffled and put facedown in a stack. Players sit side by side.

Player 1 turns over the top card and places it faceup in front of both players.

Player 2 turns over the second card. She adds the number to Player 1's, and then verbalizes the equation. Player 2 places her card faceup next to Player 1's card. Player 1 turns over the next card, and adds that number to the sum of the first two cards and verbalizes the equation. He lays the card beside the other two.

Example
Player 1 turns over a 4. Player 2 turns over a 5 and says, "Four plus five equals nine." Player 1 turns over a 5 and says, "Nine plus five equals fourteen."

Play continues in this manner, with players alternating turns, until a player has a card that when added to the previous sum will result in a sum greater than 25. When that happens, the player must subtract the number from the previous sum rather than add it.

Play continues until someone gets a sum of exactly 25.

Questions

- What number do you need to hit 25 exactly?
- Which numbers will get you almost to 25 but not exactly?
- Which numbers will be too much and force you to subtract?

The Double Ladder Game

The goal of this game is to be the player to fill in more rungs of the ladder.

One-digit addition

One-digit subtraction

Kindergarten: CCSS.K.OA.A.3

Grade 1: CCSS.1.OA.C.6

Grade 2: CCSS.2.OA.B.2

Two players

Materials

- ten-frame cards
- "The Double Ladder Game" recording sheet for each player
- pencils

	Addition	Subtraction
10 =		
9 =		
8 =		
7 =		
6 =		
5 =		
4 =		
3 =		
2 =		
1 =		

How to play

The cards are shuffled and dealt. (Players take turns being the dealer.) Each player gets twelve cards. The players will use these twelve cards throughout the game. (The remaining cards are not needed and can be put aside.)

Players must use their cards to make an addition equation and a subtraction equation for each rung of the ladder. Rungs are to be filled sequentially. Each card may be used only *once* in a single equation, but players may use all their cards again for the next equation.

Player 1 searches his twelve cards for a way to fill in the first rung of his ladder. He writes both equations on the 1 = rung. Player 2 checks to make sure Player 1's equations are correct. Player 2 then searches her hand of twelve cards for a way to do the same, but she can only make one of the equations for that rung. Player 1 checks her equation for accuracy. This ends the first round of play.

Players take turns working their way up the ladder. When both players have completed making equations for the 10 rung, the player with more equations on his recording sheet is the winner.

I like this game because it sets up equations that are a reversal of the usual format and look like this: 1 = 3 − 2. Children are so used to seeing 3 − 2 = 1 that they think the other way around is incorrect. It's not! All that matters is that both sides of the equals sign have the same value and are balanced.

Questions

* What was the easiest thing about playing this game? The hardest?
* Look at your twelve cards. Are there any other ways you could have equaled _____?

<u>Variation:</u> The game is played in the same manner, but it can be modified in two ways: The ladder is longer with additional rungs or the ladder starts at a higher number.

The Ten-Card Game

The goal of this game is to make as many addition and subtraction combinations that equal the target number as possible.

One-digit addition

One-digit subtraction

Kindergarten: CCSS.K.OA.A.3

Grade 1: CCSS.1.OA.C.6

Grade 2: CCSS.2.OA.B.2

Two players

Materials

- ten-frame cards

- one set of operations cards for each player

+	+	+
+	+	+
−	−	−
−	−	−

How to play

Every round of this game is played for a specific amount of time (five minutes, ten minutes, and so on) determined by the teacher or parent. The cards are shuffled and dealt. (Players take turns being the dealer.) Each player gets ten cards. The players will use these ten cards throughout the game. Players lay their cards faceup. The rest of the cards are placed in a facedown stack.

Player 1 turns over the top card from the facedown stack. This number becomes the target number. Players use their ten cards and the operations cards to make addition and subtraction combinations that equal the target number. A card can only be used once each turn. All ten cards may be used again in the next round.

Example
The target number is 5. Player 1's ten cards are 4 ,7, 2, 6, 9, 5, 1, 8, 2, and 4. She makes the following addition and subtraction combinations: 1 + 4, 9 − 4 (she can use two 4s, because she was dealt two 4 cards), and 7 − 2.

At the end of the specified time, the children are told to stop. Players check each other's combinations for accuracy. Players get one point for each combination that equals the target number.

The target card is placed at the bottom of the facedown stack. Player 2 turns over the top card for a new target number for the next round. Each round has its own target number, and players alternate turning over the top card. At the end of five rounds, the player with more points wins the game.

Questions

- I see that you have addition combinations. Are there any remaining numbers that you could use to create subtraction combinations?

- What was easy about this game? What was more difficult?

Variation: Two cards are turned over. Players add them together in their heads to get the target number. They use their ten cards and the operations cards to make addition and subtraction combinations that equal the target number. For example, a 7 and a 6 are turned over. Players use their cards to create combinations that will equal 13.

Benchmark Numbers

The goal of this game is to find two cards that are of equal value.

Two-digit addition

Two-digit subtraction

Grade 1

Grade 2: CCSS.2.NBT.B.5

Two players

Materials

- "Benchmark Numbers" cards

75 + 25	50 + 50	50 + 25	100 − 25
60 + 40	10 + 90	25 + 25	85 − 10
51 + 49	95 + 5	100 − 50	20 + 5
75 − 25	51 − 1	65 + 10	30 + 20
1 + 24	10 + 15	45 + 5	26 − 1
35 − 10	50 − 25	74 + 1	76 − 1

Pregame

The practice session with the cards *faceup* allows the children to see what they are expected to do mathematically.

The cards are shuffled and placed faceup in a grid of six rows with four cards in each row.

Player 1 picks up one card and says the fact out loud to the other player. He then finds another card that equals the sum or difference of the first and verbalizes that fact, too. If Player 1 has chosen correctly, he keeps the two cards because they both have the same value.

Example

Player 1 selects 50 + 25 and says, "Fifty plus twenty-five equals seventy-five. I am looking for another card that equals seventy-five." He finds 100 − 25 and says, "One hundred minus twenty-five equals seventy-five."

Player 2 selects a card and play proceeds in the same manner. Players alternate turns until all the cards are matched.

Multiple Operations

When playing this game, players may need paper and a pencil to calculate the addition and subtraction equations on the cards.

How to play

The cards are shuffled and placed *facedown* in a grid of six rows with four cards in each row.

Player 1 turns over one card, keeping it in place, and says the fact as well as what he is looking for out loud to the other player.

Example
Player 1 turns over the 1 + 24 card. He says to Player 2, "One plus twenty-four equals twenty-five. I am looking for another card that equals twenty-five."

Player 1 turns over a second card, keeping it in place, and if it has the same value as the first card, he keeps both cards. If it doesn't, he turns both cards back over in place.

Player 2 proceeds in the same manner.

Players alternate turns until all the cards are matched. The player with more cards wins the game.

Questions

- What did you discover while playing this game?
- What was easy? What was more difficult?

Multiplication

Introduction

Glossary 180

One-Digit Multiplication

Circles and Triangles 181

Count the Points 183

Rectangles 185

Multiplication War 1 187

Multiplication War 2 188

Salute Multiplication 189

Introduction

We use multiplication frequently in our daily lives. Understanding the concepts of multiplication and memorizing multiplication facts are two very important rungs on the mathematics ladder. If children miss either rung, they will find that division, long multiplication, fractions, and algebra will be much more difficult than they should be, and they may begin to lose confidence.

Students first need to understand that multiplication can be considered in different ways: It is the grouping of sets, repeated addition, and a faster way of adding. For children who are new to the concepts of multiplication, here are two simple and straightforward ways to begin:

1. Help children visualize what happens in multiplication by using real hands-on materials that they can manipulate.

   - You must pass out four crackers to each member of your family of five. *How many crackers are needed?* How would you show what that looked like in numbers (4 + 4 + 4 + 4 + 4 = 20 [repeated addition])? Or to make it simpler, we could write 5 (people) x 4 (crackers each) = 20 crackers (multiplication).

   - You are playing a card game with six friends and each player needs five cards. *How many cards do you need to deal out?* What would that look like in numbers (5 + 5 + 5 + 5 + 5 + 5 = 30 cards [repeated addition])? Or to make it simpler, we could write 6 (friends) x 5 (cards each) = 30 cards (multiplication).

2. Next, in order to help further their understanding of the concept, have children represent their thinking by encouraging them to draw pictures.

   - There are seven tricycles. How many wheels are there all together? Draw a picture to show what that would look like. What would that look like in numbers (3 + 3 + 3 + 3 + 3 + 3 + 3 = 21 wheels)? Or we could write 7 (tricycles) x 3 (wheels each) = 21 wheels.

   - There are four plastic eggs with four chocolate candies inside each one. Draw a picture to show what that would look like. What would that look like in numbers (4 + 4 + 4 + 4 = 16 candies)? Or we could say 4 (plastic eggs) x 4 (candies in each one) = 16 candies.

Multiplication

Only after children understand the concept of multiplication, should you even consider drilling the multiplication facts.

When you drill the multiplication facts, this is the time to highlight the importance of rapid recall. Students should be aware that they must recall the answer instantly.

Understanding the concept of multiplication and memorizing the multiplication facts are facilitated by the following games. They're a great way to prepare your children for Grade 3, where multiplication is stressed.

When my granddaughter was in third grade, I helped her with her multiplication by asking questions like—

- Six cars—How many rearview mirrors? ($6 \times 3 = 18$)

- Three people—How many toes? ($3 \times 10 = 30$)

- Nine cows—How many legs? ($9 \times 4 = 36$)

- Ten people—How many noses? ($10 \times 1 = 10$)

- Two six-packs of soda—How many cans? ($2 \times 6 = 12$)

- Five skateboards—How many wheels? ($5 \times 4 = 20$)

Questions like these make multiplication more concrete and less abstract for young children.

Multiplication Glossary

When playing any math games, it is important that the children become familiar with the correct math terminology for certain facts and concepts. In this section there are two words that should be introduced and consistently used; their definitions are below.

Factor is a whole number that is multiplied with another number (factor) to make a third number (product).

Product is the amount realized when two (or more) factors are multiplied together; the answer to a multiplication problem.

factor		factor	equals sign	product
3	x	3	=	9

Circles and Triangles

The goal of the game is to make equal groups.

One-digit multiplication
Grade 2: CCSS.2.OA.C.4

Two players

Materials

- ten-frame cards, 1–6, four of each; the same if using a standard deck

- one coin

- pencils

- "Circles and Triangles" recording sheet for each player

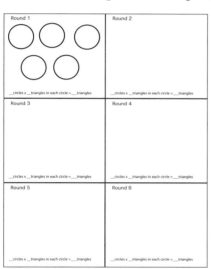

How to play

The cards are shuffled and placed facedown in a stack.

Player 1 takes a card and draws that number of circles in the Round 1 box on his recording sheet. Player 2 takes a card and proceeds in the same manner.

Player 1 takes a second card and puts that number of triangles inside *each* circle. Player 2 takes a second card and proceeds in the same manner.

Example
Player 1 takes a 5 for his first card and draws five circles in the Round 1 box. For his second card, Player 1 gets a 3. He draws three triangles inside each circle.

Round 1	Round 2
 ___circles x ___triangles in each circle = ___triangles	 ___circles x ___triangles in each circle = ___triangles
Round 3 ___circles x ___triangles in each circle = ___triangles	Round 4 ___circles x ___triangles in each circle = ___triangles
Round 5 ___circles x ___triangles in each circle = ___triangles	Round 6 ___circles x ___triangles in each circle = ___triangles

Each player writes a multiplication equation that reflects—

* how many circles were drawn;

* how many triangles were put in each circle; and

* how many triangles are in all of the circles.

Players read their equations to each other.

Player 1 flips a coin:

* **If it comes up heads,** the player with more triangles wins the round.

* **If it comes up tails,** the player with fewer triangles wins the round.

The four used cards are put in a discard pile. If the facedown cards run out, the discard pile is shuffled, placed facedown in a stack, and play continues.

The players alternate drawing first to start each round; that is, Player 2 starts round 2 by taking the first card; Player 1 starts round 3 by taking the first card.

Questions

* Why did you end up with more (or less) than the other player?

* Can you explain to me why _____ x _____ = _____?

* What card could you have drawn that would have given you more (or less) than the other player?

<u>Variations:</u> As the children get more familiar with the game, it can be expanded by adding the 7s, then 8s, and so forth, to the card deck.

Count the Points

The goal of the game is to add the products and get the greatest sum.

One-digit multiplication
Grade 2: CCSS.2.OA.C.4

Two players

Materials

- ten-frame cards 1–5, four of each;
  the same if using a standard deck

- paper

- pencils

How to play

The cards are shuffled and placed facedown in a stack.

Player 1 takes a card and draws that number of vertical lines. Player 2 takes a card and does the same.

Player 1 takes a second card and draws that number of horizontal lines crisscrossing the vertical lines. Player 2 takes a second card and does the same. Both players draw dots at the points of intersection between the two sets of lines. Each player writes the multiplication equation illustrated by the grid under it. This product is recorded as the player's score for that round.

In this game, the children draw a visual model of multiplication, and then write the equation, mentally moving from a concrete representation to an abstract number sentence.

Example
Player 1 turns over a 4 for his first card and draws four vertical lines.

For his second card, Player 1 turns over a 3 and draws three horizontal lines crisscrossing the vertical lines.

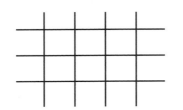

Player 1 draws dots at the points of intersection between the two sets of lines on his paper. He has three rows with four points in each row, and writes the equation, 4 x 3 = 12. He scores twelve points for this round.

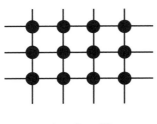

$$4 \times 3 = 12$$

Players alternate turns. After six rounds, players add the products for each round. The player with the greater sum wins the game.

This is a great strategy for helping children calculate multiplication problems fairly quickly. I find that students often create this grid when they don't know the answer to a specific multiplication problem. It may be especially helpful while playing some of these multiplication games and in testing situations.

Questions

- Why does this work?
- Is there another way to create a "picture" of _____?
- Will this work for every multiplication problem?

Variation: The game is played in the same way, but using cards 1 to 10, four of each.

Rectangles

The goal of this game is to fit as many rectangles as possible within a 12 by 12 grid. Points are scored by finding the areas of the rectangles.

One-digit multiplication
Grade 2: CCSS.2.OA.C.4

Two players

Materials

- ten-frame cards 1–6, four of each;
  the same if using a standard deck

- "Rectangles" 12 by 12 grid for each player

- pencils

- crayons

How to play

The rules for drawing the rectangles are explained to the players:
- All rectangles must be placed entirely within the 12 by 12 grid.
- The edges of rectangles may touch, but they do not have to.
- Rectangles may not overlap each other.
- No rectangle may be placed inside another rectangle.

The cards are shuffled and placed facedown in a stack.

Player 1 takes two cards. She constructs a rectangle by marking its width on a horizontal line of the grid using the number on one card and marking its height on a vertical line using the number on the other card.

Player 1 then writes the equation inside that rectangle, colors it, and calculates her score by determining the number of squares within the rectangle.

Example
Player 1 takes a 4 and a 5. She draws a 4 x 5 rectangle anywhere she wants on the grid paper, keeping the rules in mind. She writes the equation 4 x 5 = 20 in the rectangle and colors the rectangle. Her score is twenty.

Player 2 takes two cards and proceeds in the same manner. Players continue to alternate turns.

If a player takes two cards that will result in a rectangle that will not fit on his grid, that player is out of the game. He adds all the products of the rectangles in his grid. This is his score for the game.

The game ends when both players can no longer build rectangles on their grids. The player with the highest score wins.

Questions

- What did you discover while playing this game?

- When you play it a second time, will you do anything differently? What?

- Is it better to get numbers that are greater or smaller? Why or why not?

- Which made the difference in scores—more rectangles or bigger rectangles?

Variation: "Bigger Rectangles" is played using ten-frame cards 1 to 10 and the "Bigger Rectangles" 24 by 24 grid.

Multiplication War 1

The goal of this game is to have the greatest product.

One-digit multiplication
Grade 2: CCSS.2.OA.C.4

Two players

Materials

- ten-frame cards 1–5, four of each; the same if using a standard deck

How to play

Players sit side by side. The multiplication fact to practice is chosen by the adult or the players and one card with that factor (number) is placed between the two players. The cards are shuffled and placed facedown in a stack.

Both players take one card. Each player multiplies her number by the constant factor in the middle. Players must verbalize their equations.

If the players don't verbalize their equations, they don't really have to do any multiplication. They will merely take the cards based on who draws the greater number.

The player with the greater product collects both cards.

Example
It is decided to practice "times 3," so one 3 is placed between the two players. Player 1 draws a 4; Player 2 draws a 2. Players multiply their numbers by 3, and express their equations out loud: "Four times three equals twelve"; "Two times three equals six." Player 1 has the greater product so he collects both cards.

If both players have the same product (a tie), each player takes one more card, lays it on top of the first card, and multiplies it by the constant factor. The player with the greater product wins all four cards.

When all the cards in the facedown stack have been used, players count their cards. The player with the most cards wins the game.

Questions

- I see you have _____ times _____ and you are not sure what the answer is. What can you do to help yourself?

- Have you figured out what you already know well and what you need to practice?

- Explain why you both have different factors but have the same product.

Variations: The game is played the same way, but cards 1 to 6 are used. As the children become familiar with this version, add the 7 cards to the game, and so on.

Multiplication War 2

The goal of the game is to draw two factors that when multiplied together have the greatest product.

One-digit multiplication
Grade 2: CCSS.2.OA.C.4

Two players

Materials

- ten-frame cards 0–5, four of each,
  or a standard deck 1–5, four of each

How to play

The cards are shuffled and placed facedown in a stack.

Player 1 takes two cards. He multiplies the factors (numbers) and verbalizes the equation; for example, "Four times five equals twenty."

Player 2 takes two cards. She multiplies the factors and verbalizes the equation; for instance, "Three times four equals twelve."

The player with the greatest product collects all four cards. In case of a tie, each player takes two more cards and multiplies the factors. The player with the greater product collects all eight cards.

When all the facedown cards have been used, the players count their accumulated cards. The player with the most cards is the winner.

It is very important that players verbalize their equations. If they don't they may not do the multiplication. They may merely recognize that one player has greater factors and take the four cards based on that fact.

If a player cannot multiply two factors because she does not have the product in instant recall, encourage her to use pencil and paper to figure it out. Don't give her the answer. One effective way of figuring it out is the tactic used in the "Count Your Points" game (page 183).

Questions

- What did you notice about factors and products when you played the game?

- Why was your product greater than or less than the other player's product?

- Why is it that you both had different factors but the same products?

Variations: As children gain proficiency at playing this game, it can be expanded to include the 6s as factors, then eventually the 7s, and so on.

Salute Multiplication

The goal of this game is to discover the unknown factor.

One-digit multiplication with a missing factor
Grade 2: CCSS.2.OA.C.4

Two players

Materials

- ten-frame cards 1–5, four of each;
  the same if using a standard deck

How to play

The cards are shuffled and placed facedown in a stack.

Player 1 takes the top card and places it faceup for all to see, and states the factor out loud.

Player 2 takes a card but **does not look at it.** Player 2 holds the card on her forehead so that Player 1 can see it, but she can't.

Player 1 *mentally* multiplies the two factors and says out loud, "_____ times the factor on your head equals _____."

Player 2 listens and figures out what the unknown factor on her head must be and says that factor out loud.

Example
Player 1 turns over a 3 for all to see. Player 2 puts a 4 on her forehead without looking at it. Player 1 mentally multiplies the two factors and says, "Three times the factor on your head equals twelve." Player 2 must figure out what factor times three equals twelve. She says, "I must have a 4 on my head because three times four equals twelve."

If the first response is correct, Player 2 gets one point. If it isn't correct, she must do something that will help her figure it out, such as draw a picture, use counters, or use the strategy in "Count the Points" (page 183), but she does not receive a point for this round.

Players reverse roles and play continues until one player has ten points.

Questions

- You can't figure out what the factor on top of your head is. What can you do to help yourself?

- What multiplication fact do you already know that might be able to help you?

- Which multiplication facts do you already know? Which ones do you need to practice?

<u>Variations:</u> As children gain proficiency at playing this game with numbers 1 to 5 as factors, it can be expanded to include the 6s, then eventually the 7s, and so on.

The Games

Money

Introduction

Activities

Free Exploration of Coins 192

Alike and Different with a Magnifying Glass 193

Identifying Coins

Found a Coin 194

Coin Collector 195

Coin Values: Pennies and Nickels

Race to Five Nickels 196

Counting Nickels 197

Coin Values: Pennies and Dimes

Race to Five Dimes 198

Race to Ten Dimes 199

Rocket to $1.00 201

Counting Dimes 203

Coin Values: Pennies, Nickels, and Dimes

Race to Five Dimes Using Pennies and Nickels 204

50¢ 205

Coin Values: Pennies, Nickels, Dimes, and Quarters

Race to a Quarter 207

Counting Quarters 208

Which Is Worth More? 209

73¢ 210

Introduction

There are no standards for the teaching of money in kindergarten and first grade in the Common Core State Standards for Mathematics. But even these young children can learn about money using the following easy activities and games.

We no longer use coins and paper currency as much as we used to. Debit, credit, and gift cards have become the standard method of exchange. However, children still need to be able to count money and make change. The very best way for them to learn about money is to use the real thing!

Parents, consider giving your young children a small allowance for those little extras they see and want. Part of learning is practicing. Let your children make the purchasing decisions with their own money. Let them pay for the gum or candy or small toy they want. Even if you don't agree with their spending choices, it's okay. By letting them learn from their mistakes when the stakes aren't high, they will become better money managers in the long run. And they'll gain experience counting out bills and coins and making change.

Teachers, I'm not talking about pictures of money in a workbook or the plastic money most schools use to teach money! No, I'm talking real pennies, nickels, dimes, and quarters and faux paper money for classroom use.

Children will use that plastic stuff if they have to, but give them some real coins, and interest and engagement soar!

However, I know that most teachers are concerned about two issues:

1. Teachers spend money on their classrooms all the time. It's true that it is a hefty little investment to get enough pennies, nickels, dimes, and quarters for an entire class to play some of the following money games. (I invested about $80.00.) But that money will still be there the day you retire. The money you spent on crayons, borders, and other supplies will not. Think of it as a nest egg!

2. Most teachers worry that some children will "borrow" the coins. I learned that no matter the socioeconomic level of the children, a few children will "borrow." I sat "my" children down and told them I knew them well enough to know that they were good kids and that I trusted them completely. Because of that trust, I was going to let them use some of my money. Only once in many years of teaching was that trust shaken. On the day I retired, I counted my nest egg, and discovered that I actually had more money than I had started with. Children would bring in money they found on the playground and put it in our stash!

Activities

Before beginning some of these great games, give the following two activities a try.

Free Exploration of Coins

Give the children a small tub of real coins and give them time to dig in and inspect the coins. This might be a good time for you to watch and note what is happening:

- Do some of them already know the names of each coin?
- Do they know the values?
- Do they notice likenesses and differences?
- Do they sort the coins?
- Do they make patterns, such as penny, nickel, penny, nickel; or dime, dime, quarter, dime, dime, quarter?

Alike and Different with a Magnifying Glass

Children need to be able to identify coins before they can learn their values. This activity gives children the opportunity to examine pennies, nickels, dimes, and quarters closely and to think about what things are the same and different among them. **It is important for young learners to be able to notice likenesses and differences, especially in math and reading.**

You will need a magnifying glass and a penny, nickel, dime, and quarter for each child.

Allow the children to experiment with a magnifying glass first. Distribute the pennies, one to each child. Have them look at it closely and tell you what they notice. Begin with the "heads" side. Do they see the year and the place the coin was minted? What are the other words on the coin? What else do they see? Then have them look at the "tails" side, and don't forget to examine the edges. Ask the children to draw a picture of both sides of each coin.

Have them look closely at each coin in turn, noting how the coins are alike and different. You might draw a vertical line down the board or paper to create two columns, and write "Alike" at the top of one and "Different" at the top of the other.

Encourage the children to talk about what things are the same and those that are different. Some things appear on every coin; some do not. What do they notice about size and value?

Now everyone is ready to play the games.

Money

Found a Coin

The goal of this game is to help children identify coins by attributes and name.

Identifying coins
Kindergarten

Two players

Materials

- a small paper bag containing five of each coin
- "Found a Coin" game board for each player

Penny	Nickel	Dime	Quarter

How to play

Before beginning the game, players should trace the shape of each coin above its name on their game boards.

Player 1 reaches into the bag and, without looking, pulls out a coin. He places the coin in the appropriate box on his board and identifies the coin out loud; for example, "This is a dime." (Coins drawn more than once should be stacked on the board.)

Player 2 reaches into the bag, pulls out a coin, and proceeds in the same manner.

Players alternate turns until there are no more coins in the paper bag. Players then record the number of pennies, nickels, dimes, and quarters they have.

Questions

- What is the value of your pennies? Nickels? Dimes? Quarters?

Coin Collector

The object of this game is to collect pennies, nickels, dimes, and quarters.

Identifying coins
Kindergarten
Grade 1
Grade 2: CCSS.2.MD.C.8

Two players

Materials

- tub of pennies, nickels, dimes, and quarters
- ten-frame cards 1–4, four of each;
  the same if using a standard deck
- "Coin Collector" draw/take chart

Draw	Take
1	Penny
2	Nickel
3	Dime
4	Quarter

How to play

The cards are shuffled and placed facedown in a stack.

Player 1 draws a card and takes a coin according to the Draw/Take Chart. Player 2 draws a card and proceeds in the same manner.

The players alternate turns until both players have twenty coins. They count each denomination and compare their numbers of pennies, nickels, dimes, and quarters. The player who has more of one type gets a point. For instance, Player 1 has 4 pennies and Player 2 has 6 pennies. Player 2 gets a point because she has more pennies.

Questions

- If you play this game again, do you think you will get exactly the same amount of pennies, nickels, dimes, and quarters? Try it and see.
- What is the value of your pennies? Nickels? Dimes Quarters?
- How much are all your coins worth?
- Who has more money? Less? How do you know?

Race to Five Nickels

The goal of this game is to be the first player to collect five nickels.

Trading pennies for nickels
Kindergarten
Grade 1
Grade 2: CCSS.2.MD.C.8

Two players

Materials

- ten-frame cards 1–4, four of each;
  the same if using a standard deck

- tub of coins

How to play

Have the children sort the coins. The only coins needed for this game are the pennies and nickels. The dimes and quarters are set aside.

The cards are shuffled and placed facedown in a stack.

Player 1 draws a card and takes that number of pennies. She puts the card in a discard pile. Player 2 draws a card and proceeds in the same manner.

The players alternate turns. When the facedown cards are gone, the cards in the discard pile are shuffled, stacked facedown, and play continues.

When a player has five or more pennies, he should trade five of those pennies for a nickel. The first player to collect five nickels wins the game.

Questions

- How many more pennies do you need to be able to trade for another nickel?

- I see you have [any number more than five] pennies. Do you have enough to trade for a nickel? Will you trade all of them?

Variation 1: The game is played in the same way, but at the end of each turn, the players tell each other how much money they have accumulated thus far in the game.

Variation 2: "Race to Ten Nickels" is played the same way, but ten-frame cards 1 to 10 are used.

You know children understand the value of a nickel when they draw a 6 and take one nickel and one penny. But the player must explain to the other player why he took one nickel and one penny instead of six pennies.

Counting Nickels

The goal is to be the first player to cross off all the nickel sums on their game board.

Counting nickel values
Kindergarten
Grade 1
Grade 2: CCSS.2.MD.C.8

Two players

Materials

- ten-frame cards with 0s removed,
  or a standard deck with face cards removed

- tub of coins

- "Counting Nickels" game board for each player

more**4U**

5¢	10¢	15¢	20¢	25¢	30¢	35¢	40¢	45¢	50¢

How to play

Draw the game board on the board, and if you wish, have the children make their own boards. This allows them to more readily notice the patterns created when skip-counting by 5s. Then allow the children to sort the coins, putting the nickels in a separate pile. Set the pennies, dimes, and quarters aside; they will not be needed.

The cards are shuffled and placed facedown in a stack. Player 1 takes one card and takes that number of nickels. Player 1 counts the nickels out loud.

Example
Player 1 draws a 3. She takes three nickels and counts out loud, "5¢, 10¢, 15¢."

Player 1 crosses off that nickel-sum on her game board and returns the nickels to the tub. She puts her card in a discard pile.

Player 2 draws a card and proceeds in the same manner.

If a player takes a card with a number whose nickel-sum has already been crossed off, that player loses a turn.

Players alternate turns until one player crosses off all the nickel-sums on her board.

Questions

- Ask the children how many nickels are in 20¢, 35¢, and so on.

- I see that you only have one nickel-sum to cross off. What number are you hoping to draw so that you can cross that nickel-sum off?

- Can you prove to me that _____ nickels equal _____?

Money

Race to Five Dimes

The object of this game is to be the first player to collect five dimes.

Trading pennies for dimes
Kindergarten
Grade 1
Grade 2: CCSS.2.MD.C.8

Two players

Materials

- ten-frame cards 1–5, four of each; the same if using a standard deck

- tub of coins

How to play

Have the children sort the coins, putting the pennies and dimes in separate piles. The nickels and quarters are set aside; they will not be needed.

The cards are shuffled and placed in a facedown stack. Player 1 draws the top card and takes that number of pennies. He puts the card in a discard pile. Player 2 draws a card and proceeds in the same manner.

Players alternate turns. When a player has ten or more pennies, she trades ten of the pennies for one dime.

The first player to collect five dimes wins.

<u>Variation 1:</u> The game is played in the same way, but at the end of each turn, the players tell each other how much money they have accumulated thus far in the game.

<u>Variation 2:</u> "Race to Ten Dimes" is played in the same manner using ten-frame cards 1 to 10.

Questions

- How many more pennies do you need to be able to trade for another dime?

- I see you have [any number more than ten] pennies. Do you have enough to trade for a dime?

Race to Ten Dimes

The goal is to accumulate ten dimes and reach 100. The winner trades the ten dimes for a $1 bill. (This is not an "exact" game, so players may accumulate more than 100 pennies.)

Trading pennies for dimes
Kindergarten
Grade 1
Grade 2: CCSS.2.MD.C.8

Two players

Materials

- tub of coins and one $1 bill
- one die
- hundred board for each player

1	2	3	4	5	6	7	8	9	10
11	12	13	14	15	16	17	18	19	20
21	22	23	24	25	26	27	28	29	30
31	32	33	34	35	36	37	38	39	40
41	42	43	44	45	46	47	48	49	50
51	52	53	54	55	56	57	58	59	60
61	62	63	64	65	66	67	68	69	70
71	72	73	74	75	76	77	78	79	80
81	82	83	84	85	86	87	88	89	90
91	92	93	94	95	96	97	98	99	100

How to play

Have the children sort the coins, putting the pennies and dimes in separate piles. The nickels and quarters are set aside; they will not be needed.

Player 1 rolls the die and takes that number of pennies. He puts the pennies sequentially on his hundred board, starting at 1. Player 1 tells the other player the value of the pennies on his board.

Example
Player 1 rolls a 5 and takes five pennies. He puts them on his board from 1 to 5, and says, "I have five cents."

Player 2 rolls the die and proceeds in the same manner.

When a player has put ten or more pennies on his board, he should trade ten of the pennies for a dime, and place the dime on the appropriate number.

Example
Player 1 rolls a 6 and takes six pennies. He puts them on his board. He now has eleven pennies on his board. He trades the first ten for a dime that goes on the 10, and tells his partner that he now has eleven cents.

The first player to accumulate ten dimes and reach 100 trades the ten dimes for a $1 bill and wins the game. This is not an "exact" game, so players may have more than 100.

Questions

- How many dimes does it take to make _____¢?

- What is the value of all your coins on the board right now?

- How much more will it take to get from where you are right now to _____? _____?

Rocket to $1.00

The goal of this game is to "build up" as closely as possible to $1.00 in seven rounds without going above the target.

Trading pennies for dimes
Grade 1
Grade 2: CCSS.2.MD.C.8

Two players

Materials

- one die
- tub of coins
- "Rocket to $1.00" game board for each player

Turns	Dimes	Pennies
7		
6		
5		
4		
3		
2		
1		

How to play

Have the children sort the coins, separating the pennies and dimes into separate piles. The nickels and quarters are set aside; they will not be needed. Play is limited to seven turns. To reinforce the idea of "building up" for the children, the game starts at the bottom of the game board.

Player 1 rolls the die and decides whether to add that number of dimes *or* that number of pennies to his board.

Example
Player 1 rolls a 6. He must decide whether to place six dimes or six pennies on the turn 1 line on his board and have either sixty cents or six cents after his first turn.

.

Player 2 rolls the die and proceeds in the same manner.

After any turn, players may exchange ten pennies for a dime. (This helps children see when they are getting close to $1.00.)

After each player has taken seven turns, the player closest to $1.00 without going above the target is the winner.

It is useful to play this game many times. The repetition will help the children develop strategies for winning. Thinking ahead and planning are two of those life skills that is very necessary for success.

Questions

- What is the value of the coins that you have on the board right now?

- How far from $1.00 are you?

- Have you discovered a strategy that you will use for the next game? What will you do differently?

Counting Dimes

The goal is to be the first player to cross off all the dime sums on their game board.

Counting dime values
Kindergarten
Grade 1
Grade 2: CCSS.2.MD.C.8

Two players

Materials

- tub of coins
- ten-frame cards with 0s removed,
  or a standard deck with face cards removed
- "Counting Dimes" game board for each player

more**4U**

10¢	20¢	30¢	40¢	50¢	60¢	70¢	80¢	90¢	$1.00

How to play

Draw the game board on the board, and if you wish, have the children make their own boards. This allows them to more readily notice the patterns created when skip-counting by 10s. Then let the children sort the coins, putting the dimes in a separate pile. The pennies, nickels, and quarters are set aside; they will not be needed.

The cards are shuffled and placed facedown in a stack.

Player 1 turns over the top card and takes that number of dimes. Player 1 counts the dimes out loud.

Example
Player 1 turns over a 5 and takes five dimes. She counts out loud, "10¢, 20¢, 30¢, 40¢, 50¢."

Player 1 crosses off the dime sum on her game board and returns the dimes to the tub.

Player 2 turns over one card and proceeds in the same manner.

If a player turns over a dime sum that has already been crossed off, that player loses a turn.

Players alternate turns until one player crosses off all the dime sums.

Questions

- How many dimes in _____¢? _____¢? Prove it.
- I see that you only have one dime-sum to cross off. What number are you hoping to draw so that you can cross off that dime sum? How likely is it that you will draw that number?

Race to Five Dimes Using Pennies and Nickels

The goal of this game is to be the first player to collect five dimes.

Trading pennies and nickels for dimes
Kindergarten
Grade 1
Grade 2: CCSS.2.MD.C.8

Two players

Materials

- ten-frame cards 1–5, four of each; the same if using a standard deck

- tub of coins

How to play

Have the children sort the coins into separate piles of pennies, nickels, and dimes. The quarters are set aside; they will not be needed.

The cards are shuffled and placed in a facedown stack. Player 1 draws the top card and takes that number of pennies. If Player 1 draws a 5, he takes five pennies, and then trades them for a nickel. He puts the card in a discard pile.

If after drawing a 5 a player picks up a nickel, you know that he understands the value of a nickel. However, he must explain to the other player why he can do this.

Player 2 takes a card and proceeds in the same manner.

When a player has two nickels, they are traded for one dime.

Players alternate turns. When the facedown cards are gone, the discard pile is shuffled and placed facedown in a stack. Play continues.

The first player to collect five dimes wins.

Questions

- Look at the coins you have right now. Do you see any coins that need to be traded?
- What coins do you need in order to make another trade?

Variation 1: The game is played the same way, but at the end of each turn, the players tell each other how much money they have accumulated thus far in the game.

Variation 2: The game is played the same way, but if a player forgets to make a trade, the other player takes the money earned from the last turn.

50¢

The goal of this game is to get as close to 50¢ as possible. This is not an "exact" game, so players may accumulate more than 50¢.

Using and trading pennies, nickels, and dimes
Grade 1
Grade 2: CCSS.2.MD.C.8

Two players

Materials

- tub of coins
- ten-frame cards 1–3, four of each; the same if using a standard deck
- "50¢" draw/take chart

Draw	Take
1	Penny
2	Nickel
3	Dime

How to play

Have the children sort the coins into separate piles of pennies, nickels, and dimes. The quarters are set aside; they will not be needed.

The cards are shuffled and placed in a facedown stack. Player 1 draws the top card and takes the coin indicated by the number on the card. He must verbalize which coin he has taken and its value. The card is then put in a discard pile.

Example
Player 1 draws a 2 and takes a nickel. He says, "I have a nickel, and it is worth 5¢."

Player 2 draws a card and proceeds in the same manner.

When players have five pennies or two nickels, they are expected to trade them for the appropriate coin. As play continues, the players must state how many of each coin and the value of the coins they have accumulated thus far in the game.

Example
"I have two dimes, one nickel, and two pennies, and they are worth twenty-seven cents."

Players alternate turns. When the facedown cards are gone, the discard pile is shuffled, placed facedown in a stack, and play continues.

A player may choose to stop drawing cards at any time. The player closest to 50¢ is the winner.

Example
Player 1 has 47¢. Player 2 has 52¢. Player 2 wins the game because 52 is closer to 50 than 47.

Questions

- How much more do you have than the other player?

- Can you prove to me that you have _____ cents?

- How much more do you need to get to 50¢?

- You're at _____ cents. If you draw another card, what do you hope that number will be? What are your chances of drawing that number?

- How close to 50¢ are you? How did you figure it out?

Variation: The game is the same, but it is played to get closest to $1.00.

Race to a Quarter

The goal of this game is to be the first player to take the quarter.

Trading pennies, nickels, and dimes for one quarter
Grade 1
Grade 2: CCSS.2.MD.C.8

Two players

Materials

- tub of pennies, nickels, dimes, and one quarter
- ten-frame cards 1–5, four of each,
  or the same if using a standard deck

How to play

The cards are shuffled and placed in a facedown stack. Player 1 draws the top card and takes that number of pennies. If Player 1 draws a 5, he takes five pennies, and then trades them for a nickel. He then puts the card in a discard pile.

Player 2 draws a card and proceeds in the same manner.

Players alternate turns. When the facedown cards are gone, the discard pile is shuffled and placed facedown in a stack. Play continues. Players are expected to make trades for nickels and dimes when they can.

The winner is the first player to trade two dimes and one nickel for a quarter.

Questions

- I see you have three dimes. How much is that worth? How much is a quarter worth? What could you do to trade the three dimes for a quarter?

<u>Variation 1:</u> The game is played in the same way, but at the end of each turn, the players tell each other how much money they have accumulated thus far in the game.

<u>Variation 2:</u> The goal of the game is changed to being the first player to have two, three, or four quarters ($1.00).

<u>Variation 3:</u> The game is played the same way, but if a player fails to make a trade, the other player takes the money earned from the last turn.

Counting Quarters

The goal is to be the first player to cross off all the quarter sums on the game board.

Money
Grade 1
Grade 2: CCSS.2.MD.C.8

Two players

Materials

- ten-frame cards with 0s removed,
  or a standard deck with face cards removed

- tub of coins

- "Counting Quarters" game board for each player

25¢	50¢	75¢	$1.00	$1.25	$1.50	$1.75	$2.00	$2.25	$2.50

How to play

Draw the game board on the board, and if you wish, have the children make their own boards. This allows them to more readily notice the patterns created when skip-counting by 25s. Then let the children sort the coins into a separate pile of quarters. The pennies, nickels, and dimes are set aside; they will not be needed.

The cards are shuffled and placed facedown in a stack. Player 1 turns over one card and takes that number of quarters. Player 1 counts the quarters out loud. Player 1 crosses off that quarter-sum on her game board, and puts the card in a discard pile.

Example
Player 1 turns over a 3 and takes three quarters. She counts out loud, "Twenty-five cents, fifty cents, seventy-five cents." She crosses off 75¢ on her game board, and puts the card in a discard pile.

Player 2 turns over the next card and proceeds in the same manner.

If a player turns over a quarter-sum already crossed off, that player loses his turn.

Players alternate turns. When the facedown cards are gone, the discard pile is shuffled, placed facedown in a stack, and play continues. The first player to cross off all her quarter-sums wins.

Questions

- What is the value of four quarters? Can you prove it?

- How many quarters are there in $1.25? $2.25?

Which Is Worth More?

The goal of this game is to have the coin with the greatest value.

Comparing the values of coins
Grade 1
Grade 2: CCSS.2.MD.C.8

Two players

Materials

- one die

- ten-frame cards 1–4, four of each;
  the same if using a standard deck

- "Which Is Worth More?" draw/take chart

Draw	Take
1	Penny
2	Nickel
3	Dime
4	Quarter

How to play

The cards are shuffled and placed in a facedown stack. Player 1 draws a card and takes the coin indicated by the number on the card. She verbalizes which coin was taken and its value.

Example
Player 1 draws a 2 and takes a nickel. She says, "A nickel is worth 5¢."

Player 2 takes a card and proceeds in the same manner. The player who has the coin of greater value takes both coins.

If both players have the same coin (a tie), each player takes one more card and the coin indicated. The player whose two coins have the greater combined value takes all four coins.

Play continues until the facedown stack of cards has been depleted. The winner is the player who has the most coins or whose money has the greater value.

Questions

- Convince me that you have _____ cents.

- Who has more? How much more? How did you figure it out?

- What number are you hoping to draw? What are the chances of drawing that number?

Money

73¢

Using pennies, nickels, dimes, and quarters, players try to force the other player to add the last coin to make the total *exactly* 73¢. The player who adds the last coin loses the game.

Adding coin values
Grade 1
Grade 2: CCSS.2.MD.C.8

Two players

Materials

- paper plate
- tub of pennies, nickels, dimes, and quarters

This is one of my very favorite games. Children love it and get lots of experience counting and totaling coin amounts. This is also a game of strategy. The more they play, the better children are able to think ahead and make plans for what they intend to do next.

How to play

The paper plate is placed between the two players. Player 1 chooses any coin and places it on the paper plate. He states the value of the money.

Example
Player 1 puts a dime on the paper plate and says, "I put in a total of ten cents."

Player 2 chooses any coin and also places it on the plate. Player 2 must add the value of the two coins and state how much money is now in the plate.

Example
Player 2 puts a nickel on the plate and says, "Now there is fifteen cents."

Players alternate turns, adding one coin at a time and totaling the amount of money in the paper plate. The winner is the player who forces the other player to add the last coin to total 73¢.

When children first begin to play this game, it will probably take them considerable time and effort to count the value of the coins in the paper plate each time. This is completely normal. The more they do it, the better they will get.

Questions

- Have you discovered any helpful strategies?

- What will you do differently in the next game?

- How did you figure out the total value of the coins in the paper plate?

- You are at sixty-three cents. What coins can you safely add to the paper plate? Why?

Variation 1: The game is played in exactly the same manner, but the player who adds the last coin to total exactly 73¢ wins.

Variation 2: The game is played to different money amounts; for instance, 47¢ or 91¢.

Money

The Games

Fractions

Introduction

Glossary 214

Activity

Fraction Kit 215

Games

Cover 217

Uncover 218

Fraction War 219

Introduction

Children come to kindergarten with a rudimentary understanding of basic fraction concepts. I learned this early on when I showed my kindergarten class a big cookie and told them I was going to divide it in half—half for me and half for one of them. I cut the cookie into one big piece for me and one little piece for one of them. "That's not fair!" they immediately cried. "Why is it unfair?" I asked. "Because it needs to be exactly the same for both of you," they responded. They were right. **Fractions represent equal parts of a whole.**

The Common Core State Standards introduce fractions in the third grade (NGA Center and CCSSO 2010, p. 22). However, even younger children have some knowledge of fractions and can understand the concept if you begin with concrete experiences.

Use the term *equal sharing* and real objects to introduce fractions.

- I have one brownie and the two of you will be sharing it equally. How much brownie will each of you get?

- I have one brownie and the four of you will be sharing it equally. How much brownie will each of you get?

- I have two brownies and the three of you will be sharing it equally. How much brownie will each of you get?

Next, introduce representational thinking by having children draw pictures to further help their understanding of the concept.

- Four children want to share a candy bar so that each child gets the same amount. How much of the candy bar should each child get? Draw a picture.

- I have one pizza to share with eight people and I want everyone to get the same amount. Draw a picture to show how much each person gets.

Sharing situations provide a useful starting point for introducing fraction names, especially because some children think that fractional parts are all called *one half*.

This book includes two games that are useful for children in kindergarten through second grade because they begin with a concrete experience—making the "fraction kit." I strongly recommend that the children make the "Fraction Kit," and then play "Cover" and "Uncover." Follow up by trying a very simple version of "Fraction War."

Fractions Glossary

When playing any math games, it is important that the children become familiar with the correct math terminology for certain facts and concepts. There are two words to consistently use when doing the activities and playing the games in this section on fractions; their definitions are below.

Numerator is the top number of a fraction. It is the number of parts you have.

Denominator is the bottom number of a fraction. It is the number of parts into which the whole is divided.

Here is a simple way to remember the fraction parts: If you forget, just think "down" for denominator.

$$\frac{\text{Numerator}}{\text{Denominator}}$$

Fraction Kit

This is one activity that leads to two amazing games that really help children understand the concept of fractions. It takes some work beforehand to get ready for the games, but it is well worth the time and effort. You may be tempted to help your children by doing the preparatory work. Don't. Let them do it. Making the kits is a learning experience, too. Make sure you and the children have plenty of time to do the preliminary activity.

Fractions
Kindergarten
Grade 1
Grade 2

Materials

- one set 9 x 12-inch pieces of red, blue, green, and yellow construction paper for each child and the teacher

- scissors

- pencils

- black markers

How to play

1. Give each of the children one set of the colored construction paper, and ask them what they notice about the four pieces.

Among other things, I hope that they will notice that all four are the same size and shape—that the sheets of paper are *congruent*. Use the big word! What other objects around the home or classroom are congruent? (Paper plates are a good example.)

2. Then take the red sheet of paper and tell them to set it aside. This red piece of paper will *never* be cut. It will act as the game board for both the "Cover" and "Uncover" games. This piece of paper represents 1—the whole.

3. Take the blue sheet of paper and have the children carefully fold it in half short end to short end ("hamburger style"), open it up, and then carefully cut on the fold.

The easiest way for the children to fold the paper is to have them lay the paper on their desks or a table, fold it in half so that the corners match exactly, and then crease the paper with one hand while holding the corners together with the other hand. Sometimes young children need help, either from a peer or an adult.

- Ask them what they notice about these two pieces of paper in terms of each other. *Are these two pieces congruent?*

- Ask the children how many of these pieces fit exactly on the 1, the whole, the piece that will not be cut up.

- Using a pencil, have the children write 1/2 on both halves of the blue paper. Talk about what this means. After they have marked both pieces accurately, have them use a marker to write over the pencil lines.

4. Take the green sheet of paper and have the children carefully fold it in half short end to short end ("hamburger style"), and then in half again in the same direction. Ask them how many sections they will have on the inside when they open it up. *Were they right?* Have the children open up the green paper and carefully cut on the folds.

    - Ask them what they notice about these four pieces in terms of each other. *Are these four pieces congruent? How many fit exactly on 1/2? How many fit exactly on the whole?*

    - Have them mark 1/4 on each of the four pieces. *What does this mean?*

5. Take the yellow sheet of paper and have the children carefully fold it in half "hamburger style," and then in half again in the same direction. They then fold the sheet in half a third time in the same direction. Ask them how many sections they will have on the inside when they open it up. *Were they right?* Have the children open up the sheet and carefully cut on the folds.

    - Ask them what they notice about these eight pieces in terms of each other. *Are these eight pieces congruent? How many fit exactly on 1/4? 1/2? How many fit exactly on 1, the whole?*

    - Have them mark 1/8 on each of the eight pieces. *What does this mean?*

Now you are ready to play the two "Fraction Kit" games!

Cover

The goal of this game is to cover the board (the uncut sheet of construction paper) completely and exactly—no pieces should overlap each other or overhang the sides of the board.

Two players

Materials

- one fraction kit for each player
- one custom fraction die*
  - * Blank 1/2-inch wooden cubes are available at most education supply stores or online. Mark 1/2 on one face, 1/4 on two faces, and 1/8 on three faces with a permanent ink black marker.

How to play

Players put their red boards in front with all their fraction pieces close at hand. Player 1 rolls the die and puts that fraction piece on his board.

Player 2 rolls the die and proceeds in the same manner.

If a player rolls a fraction that cannot fit on the board, he loses that turn.

Players alternate turns until one player covers her board completely and exactly, winning the game.

Questions

- What did you notice about playing the game?
- What are you hoping to roll because you have an empty space on your board?
- Will anything else fit?
- What are your chances of rolling 1/2? 1/4? 1/8?
- When you play next time, is there anything that you will do differently?
- How would you describe what you had on your board at the end of this game?

Uncover

The goal of this game is to uncover your board (the uncut piece of construction paper) completely and exactly.

Two players

Materials

- one fraction kit for each player
- one custom fraction die*
  - * Blank 1/2-inch wooden cubes are available at most education supply stores or online. Mark 1/2 on one face, 1/4 on two faces, and 1/8 on three faces with a permanent ink black marker.

How to play

Players put their red boards in front. Players cover their boards exactly and completely using any fraction pieces they wish. For example, a player may use 1/8, 1/2, 1/4, and 1/8.

Player 1 rolls the die and takes off the fraction piece indicated. Player 2 proceeds in the same manner.

Players alternate turns until one player uncovers his board, winning the game.

Questions

- What did you notice about playing the game?
- I see you rolled 1/2 but didn't have any halves on your board. Could you have removed something else?
- When you play next time, is there anything that you will do differently?

Fraction War

The goal of this game is to create a fraction with the greater value.

Comparing Fractions
Grade 2

Two players

Materials

- ten-frame cards with 0s removed
  or a standard deck with face cards removed

- "Fraction War" game board for each player

How to play

Each player finds and places a 1 card in the numerator position on his game board. This card remains in place until the end of the game.

The remaining cards are shuffled and placed facedown in a stack.

Each player draws a card and places it in the denominator position. The player with the greater value fraction takes both denominator cards. The numerator (1) stays in place.

Expect the children to be somewhat confused regarding which denominator has the greater value. While the whole number 4 is greater than the whole number 2, as denominators their values are reversed, and this is challenging for young children. When playing this game, it would be very helpful for children to have their fraction kits so that they can actually see that 1/2 is bigger than 1/4.

Play continues until all the cards in the facedown stack are used. The player with the most cards is the winner.

Questions

- Convince me that your fraction is greater than the other player's.

- What number would you need to have drawn to make your fraction greater than the other player's?

References

Duncan, Greg J., and Amy Claessens. "School Readiness and Later Achievement." *Journal of Developmental Psychology* 43, no. 6 (November 2007): 1428–1446.

Kaye, Peggy. *Games for Math: Playful Ways to Help Your Child Learn Math, from Kindergarten to Third Grade.* New York: Pantheon Books, 1988.

National Council of Teachers of Mathematics (NCTM). *Math, Fun, and Games?: Yes Way!* Reston, Va.: NCTM, n.d. http://www.nctm.org/resources/content.aspx?id=27612.

——*Principals and Standards for School Mathematics.* Reston, Va.: NCTM, 2000.

National Governors Association Center for Best Practices (NGA Center) and Council of Chief State School Officers (CCSSO). *Common Core State Standards for Mathematics. Common Core State Standards (College- and Career-Readiness Standards and K–12 Standards in English Language Arts and Math).* Washington, D.C.: NGA Center and CCSSO, 2010. http://www.corestandards.org.

National Parent Teacher Association (PTA). *Parents' Guide to Student Success: Kindergarten.* Alexandria, Va.: National PTA, 2011. http://www.pta.org/files/K%20June20.pdf.

——*Parents' Guide to Student Success: 1st Grade.* Alexandria, Va.: National PTA, 2011. http://www.pta.org/files/1st%20Grade%20June20.pdf.

—— *Parents' Guide to Student Success: 2nd Grade.* Alexandria, Va.: National PTA, 2011. http://www.pta.org/files/2nd%20Grade%20June20.pdf.

——*Guía Para Padres Para Fomentar El Éxito Escolar: Kindergarten.* Alexandria, Va.: National PTA, 2011. http://www.pta.org/files/K_spanish_HR_June30.pdf.

—— *Guía Para Padres Para Fomentar El Éxito Escolar: 1er Grado.* Alexandria, Va.: National PTA, 2011. http://www.pta.org/files/1st_Grade_spanish_HR_June30.pdf.

—— *Guía Para Padres Para Fomentar El Éxito Escolar: 2do Grado.* Alexandria, Va.: National PTA, 2011. http://www.pta.org/files/2nd_Grade_spanish_HR_June30.pdf.